FROM A
BLACK MAN'S
PERSPECTIVE

NORA SHARIFF BORDEN

SPECIAL THANKS

A special thanks to my Lord and Savior Jesus Christ for inspiring me to write this amazing book.

Thank you to my amazing husband for all your support and love in everything I do!

A special thanks to all the men who have joined me in writing this powerful book.

Stephanie Hunt, thank you for using your gifts to bring this vision to life.

Lacie Williams, thanks for your creative talents in creating this book cover.

Aishah Hassan, thanks for your support in formatting this book.

Thank you, Amelia Winkle and Karen Brown, for using your gifts to edit this powerful book.

A special thanks to all of the men who choose to purchase this powerful and life-changing book.

INTRODUCTION

With all that is going on in the world with our black men, I felt the need to share my thoughts. I especially want to share these amazing stories from these powerful men. There are so many things that our black men have to go through to be successful and to feel good about who they are - all while living in a society that continues to oppress them and keep them down. Some are stronger than others and are able to rise above the racism. Our young boys need to see more black men succeeding in their lives as an example! They need to see more black lawyers, police officers, judges, district attorneys, investors, mayors, governors, and other great professionals.

Recently, I watched a movie called "The Banker." These two men were very smart businessmen. Their desire was not only for them to become successful for themselves and to provide a great life for their families, but to help other black men do the same. Unfortunately, because of the color of their skin, they were denied opportunities that white men were allowed! They had a good friend, who was white, purchase properties and banks in their names to position them to be successful and help others who look like them to do the same. They had to do all of this because they were not allowed to rise to the same level of success because of the color of their skin.

It is so sad, because God created us all equal regardless of race. We have made it all about race and not about God. There are those who have come along and said, "Enough is enough!" We will rise up and be who God has called us to be. We will speak up against injustice and make people accountable for their actions on all levels. We must know that we will never understand what it is like to be a race other than our own. We can, however, work towards treating everyone as one human race and treating each other with respect. I read something recently that I thought was profound.

Almost eight years after Barack Obama's election as the nation's first black president – an event that engendered a sense of optimism among many Americans about the future of race relations – a series of flashpoints around the U.S. has exposed deep racial divides and reignited a national conversation about race. A new Pew Research Center survey finds profound differences between black and white adults in their views on racial discrimination, barriers to black progress and the prospects for change. Blacks, far more than whites, say black people are treated unfairly across different realms of life, from dealing with the police to applying for a loan or mortgage. And, for many blacks, racial equality remains an elusive goal.

An overwhelming majority of blacks (88%) say the country needs to continue making changes for blacks to have equal rights with whites, but 43% are skeptical that such changes will ever occur. An additional 42% of blacks believe that the country will eventually make the changes needed for blacks to have equal rights with whites, and just 8% say the country has already made the necessary changes.

A much lower share of whites (53%) say the country still has work to do for blacks to achieve equal rights with whites, and only 11% express doubt that these changes will come. Four in ten whites believe the country will have equal rights, and about the same share (38%) say enough changes have already been made.

This tells me we still have a long way to go. I am so excited that these men have made a decision to stand up and be a change for their next generation! God's desire is that we become more like Him and the values He has set up for us, and that desire is for all people - not just a select group of people.

Nora

NORA SHARIFF BORDEN

PREFACE

Did you know? According to the U.S. Department of Justice, one in three children in America is without a father in the home.

I believe reading this book will help you understand why some black men are able to deal with life more easily because of having the presence of their fathers in their life than those who didn't! I also believe that God has a plan for all of us. In Jeremiah 29:11, God reassures us that He has a plan. I believe that all we go through in life is never in vain, and there is always a purpose for every life. Most of the time, what you are going through is never for you, but for someone else. Greatness is inside every black man, young or old. The key point is to be willing to allow God to do what He does best. When you do that, you will understand the power of God within you! God will change the lives of every person that comes before Him seeking His help. You will read some amazing stories from some powerful black men. Some grew up with their fathers in their lives, and some did not. I pray that this book will be a blessing to you and will help you begin to heal and become who God has called you to be.

1 John 4:4 tells us that greater is He that is in you, than he that is in the world. This tells me that greatness awaits us.

It is important in this day and age to teach our young black boys how to think strategically. The Word of God and these stories can show you how to be strategic in your thinking!

FROM NORA'S PERSPECTIVE

"Nora shares with passion the need for Christians to realize their God-ordained gifts and talents. It is only then that one can truly begin a journey headed to a destiny of good success.

Let this book encourage you to launch forth in God."
- BISHOP CHARLES ELLIS

AGAINST ALL ODDS

Pastor Jim Feeney, Ph.D. said it best, "The story of the once childless parents Abraham and Sarah and their miracle baby Isaac, is a story of faith and trust in God against all odds, when the "natural mind" would say that the promised child was an impossibility. The vital message that comes through is: no matter what the obstacle is, you must have faith in God!"

Romans 4:16-22 NIV says, "He is the father of us all!" As it is written, "I have made you a father of many nations." He is our father in the sight of God, in whom he believed—the God who gives life to the dead and calls into being things that were not.

Against all hope, Abraham in hope believed and so became the father of many nations, just as it had been said to him, "So shall your offspring be. " Without weakening in his faith, he faced the fact that his body was as good as dead—since he was about a hundred years old—and that Sarah's womb was also dead. Yet he did not waver through unbelief regarding the promise of God, but was strengthened in his faith and gave glory to God, being fully persuaded that God had power to do what he had promised. This is why "it was credited to him as righteousness." Roman 4: 20-21 King James Version says, "He staggered not at the promise of God through unbelief; but was strong in faith, giving glory to God; And being fully persuaded that, what he had promised, he was able to perform."

It is imperative for us to realize that God is on our side!

2 Chronicles 15:7 says, "But you, take courage! Do not let your hands be weak, for your work shall be rewarded"!

I believe it is important for us to see Him with all our heart and soul!

We have to stand on who we are in God without compromise! We have to know that we can do anything - even against all odds - because God says so. One thing about God, He will never let us go into the battlefield unaware, but it is up to us what we do with the information He gives us! I want you to decide to believe God even when all odds seem to be against you!

Do you believe God is always watching you?

If so, is how you respond to others pleasing to God?

Do you feel that it's important to treat others as God treats you?

Greatness awaits you! It is up to you to step into it!

Decide today that you will believe in the power that God has placed inside of you!

"Because what real fathers do is they make a deposit in you, through which you can make a withdrawal the rest of your life."
- BISHOP TD JAKES

EVERYONE NEEDS LOVE

I read something that explains the unconditional love of God. It said, "What does the Bible say about unconditional love? God's expression of His unconditional love is found throughout the Bible and although we are commanded to repent our sins and strive towards the ways of God, He never stops loving us on our journey to Righteousness." The Bible shows us that God's unconditional love never fails and is not motivated by personal gain.

1 Peter 4:8 says, "Above all, love each other deeply, because love covers a multitude of sins."

Colossians 3:14 says, "And over all these virtues, put on love which binds them together in perfect unity."

Ephesians 2:8 says, "For it is by grace you have been saved, through faith - and this not from yourself; it is a gift from God."

I believe that God wants to show us that all we need is the love He has for us and all we have to do is seek Him to receive it. He wants us to know that He truly does love us, and that no matter what has happened in our lives, we must learn how to move on and love ourselves like He loves us. When we do that, we are healed and will know what it is to be loved by God.

Do you believe that God loves you in spite of your sin?

Do you love yourself?

Do you feel unloved because your father was unable to love you as God loves you?

Greatness awaits you! It is up to you to step into it!

Decide today that you will believe in the power that God has placed inside of you!

"Because what real fathers do is they make a deposit in you, through which you can make a withdrawal the rest of your life."
- BISHOP TD JAKES

FOND MEMORIES

It happens to everyone as they grow up. You find out who you are and what you want, and then you realize that the people you've known forever don't see things the way you do. So you keep the fond memories, but find yourself moving on. Nicholas Sparks

No one can ever take your memories from you—each day is a new beginning, make good memories every day. Catherine Pulsifer

When I think of fond memories, I think of the things that put a smile on my face. Or thinking of a loved one who is no longer here, but when I begin to think of the fond memories of them, my heart begins to flutter. That is why it is so important to create fond memories.
Nora Shariff

Fond memories are like the cocoon of a butterfly and when they develop, they are the most beautiful memory of all. Nora Shariff

I can remember being at the birth of my grandchildren—it was one of the most beautiful memories—to see the magnificent work of God come into life.
Nora Shariff

In life we can create good memories or bad memories. The beautiful thing about creating good memories is that they remind us of all that life has to offer us and all that we can create when we put our mind to it. There is a special joy in creating fond memories.

Our childhood memories are often fragments of brief moments or encounters, which together form the scrapbook of our life.

What fond memories are you creating for yourself?

Do you feel it is important to create fond memories?

What fond memories do you have that put a smile on your face?

Greatness awaits you! It is up to you to step into it!

Decide today that you will believe in the power that God has placed inside of you!

"Because what real fathers do is they make a deposit in you, through which you can make a withdrawal the rest of your life."
- BISHOP TD JAKES

FROM A BLACK MAN'S PERSPECTIVE

I was inspired by God to write this powerful piece called "From A Black Man's Perspective." When I wrote this book, I came to realize that there were many black men who didn't have their fathers in their lives, as well as a small group who did! The more I read their stories, the more I recognized the differences in their lives. Despite their circumstances, they all turned out to be powerful black men using their gifts to contribute to their families and their communities.

I quickly realized the importance of other black men reading these stories, in hopes that it would give them the push they may need in their lives. I want them to understand that with God, all things are possible. Everything we go through in life is not necessarily for us, but always to benefit someone else. I want you to know that God has greatness waiting for you.

Critical points for you to focus on in this book:
• Through these stories, you will receive hope.
• The importance of overcoming your weaknesses!
• It is vital to be an excellent example for your children to follow.

Walk in Your Greatness!

Why is it important to see things from a different prospective?

How important is it to have a father in the life of a child?

What do our young black men need the most in their lives?

How can one overcome their circumstances?

Where should young black men look for positive role models (give some examples)?

Know that greatness awaits you. All you have to do it step into it!

Decide today that you will believe in the power inside of you!

"Because what real fathers do is they make a deposit in you, through which you can make a withdrawal the rest of your life."
- BISHOP TD JAKES

GOD HAS A VISION FOR YOU

Habakkuk: 2:2 "And the Lord answered me. Write the vision make it plain on tablets, so he may run who read it."

Habakkuk: 2:3 "For still the vision awaits its appointed time: it hastens slow. Wait for it: it will surely come; it will not delay."

Jeremiah: 29:11 "For I know the plans I have for you, declares the Lord, plans for your welfare and not for evil, to give you a future and hope."

Acts 18:9 "And the Lord said to Paul one night in a vision, "Do not be afraid, but go on speaking and do not be silent."

Here God is telling us like he told Paul, that he has a vision for us. He wants us to be confident in the plans that he has for us. He does not want us to be afraid of his plans, because the plans of the Lord are great! Here are some key points we must do to bring our vision alive.

1. We must write down the vision so that it will be plain and clear.

2. Stay focused on your vision but don't get comfortable. Be willing to change if you must. With God there are always changes because He has greater things for us and we will not be able to receive them by standing in the same spot for too long. Change is not easy but it is definitely necessary!

3. It is important to have the right people in our lives. These are the people that are going in the same direction that you are going. People who are up lifting and encourage you.

4. It is important to not focus on your circumstances because your circumstances will pass but stay focused on your visions and your blessings that will last.

5. Sometimes our vision can be too small and it does not fit into the big plan that God has for us. He will stretch us to help you reach His big plans that He has for us.

What is your Vision?

Do you spend more time focused on your circumstances or your blessing?

Do you have the right people in your life?

Who do you need to let go of in your life?

Greatness awaits you! It is up to you to step into it!

Decide today that you will believe in the power that God has placed inside of you!

"Because what real fathers do is they make a deposit in you, through which you can make a withdrawal the rest of your life."
- BISHOP TD JAKES

HEALING IN THE MIDST OF PAIN

In the book of Isaiah 41:10 God says "Fear not (there is nothing to fear), for I am with you: do not look around you in terror and be dismayed, for I am your God. I will strengthen and harden you to difficulties, yes, I will help you; yes, I will hold you up and retain you with my (victorious) right hand of righteousness and justice."

When I read this scripture it reminds me of the countless conversations that my husband and I have had about the men in our lives (family and friends). Men we knew that did not grow up with their fathers in their lives and how it affected them in life. I thought about my father and how he enlisted in the army at a young age and when he returned home he was addicted to heroin, a habit that was just too strong to quit. He was in so much pain emotionally from both the trauma of the army, as well as the effects of his father's absence, that he couldn't let the drugs go. I believe that his inability to be the father that we needed was because his father was not there for him. The drugs became a substitute for the love he so desperately needed. Unfortunately, he never understood the greatness that God placed inside of him and so he died taking it to the grave with him—like many others. My great-grandfather, Archibald Fitz Allen was a young, wealthy 17 year old from Barbados, who came to the United States in 1906. He became a skilled painter and six years later met and married my great-grandmother, Nellie Mae Williams, and together they had five children. He was surprised at the amount of racism in the U.S. and did not know how to deal with the pressures this country put on men that looked like him, especially since he hadn't had to deal with racism growing up. He started drinking and ultimately became an alcoholic. Alcoholism stopped him from being the father that his children needed him to be, causing his male children to grow up not knowing how to be good fathers and becoming alcoholics themselves. What is even more sad is that my grandfather's son Aubrey Miller had four boys who also all ended up becoming alcoholics. The one thing I know for sure is that it's important to have a positive father figure in your life. These men were all smart and gifted and all they needed was a father to tell them that they could be all that they were called to be. When you don't have a Godly figure of a man in your life you get directed away from the pathway of God. The good thing is, that in spite of it all, God is still watching over us, even when we can't see. My inspiration for writing this book is to show other young, black men that they have gifts inside of them waiting to be born. And to let them know that they don't have to fail in life because of the decisions made by their fathers, not to be in their lives. Young, black men have to say to themselves at some point, that the buck stops here! And I am going to be a better person and father than my father was to me. I am so thankful that the young men in my family are growing to become who God has called them to be as men and as fathers. We have the greatest father of all, our Lord and our Savior Jesus Christ! We can take our pain and cast it at his feet, and He will take care of us.

Discovering the healing power of Christ is the key!

What hidden pain are you not dealing with?

How are you dealing with your pain?

Are you working on forgiving your father?

Greatness awaits you! It is up to you to step into it!

Decide today that you will believe in the power that God has placed inside of you!

"Because what real fathers do is they make a deposit in you, through which you can make a withdrawal the rest of your life."
- BISHOP TD JAKES

I AM MADE IN HIS IMAGE

Genesis 1:27, "So God created mankind in His own image, in the image of God He created them: male and female he created them." (NIV)

Job 33:12, "I reply to you, Behold, in this you are not just; God is superior to Man, (and Woman)" (AMPC)

He clearly shares with us the power of the spoken word. So, if we are made in His image and likeness, then there is nothing impossible for us to accomplish I think the problem is we get so caught up in what we see, which prevents us from seeing the power of God at work in us. Let me be clear with you that God is greater than all of us. Think of it this way, you get married, you have a child, and you hear people say to you, as the father he or she is made in your image, he or she looks just like you. Then you begin to shape and mold that child into greatness. We can't let the fact that we may or may not have had our fathers in our lives stop us from hearing and seeing the message of God. Let us stay focused on becoming the powerful human beings that He created us to be.

I often think about my great grandfather, Archibald Fitz Allen and the men in my family and how they allowed the fact that life did not deal them a fair deal, which caused them to not see the possibilities that God had in store for them. My great grandfather left his country as a young man in 1906 and came to the states and had to deal with the racism which he found very hard to deal with; he eventually started drinking, which ultimately took a toll his life. Just think if he had stopped and realized that he was made in the image of God, he could have set a better foundation for his own children, so that they could have done the same for their children.

What I do know is that all things work together for good. Which means that even in the midst of chaos, goodness will show up. What brings my heart joy is that God always has a greater plan, all because we are made in His image. I am so glad that I finally realize that I was made in the image of God and that there is nothing I can't do, as long as I speak it and focus on the power of God in me.

Do you believe that you are made in the image of God?

Do you trust Gods' plans for your life?

How are you following what God has for you (if you have your father in your life or If you don't have your father in your life)?

Greatness awaits you! It is up to you to step into it!

Decide today that you will believe in the power that God has placed inside of you!

"Because what real fathers do is they make a deposit in you, through which you can make a withdrawal the rest of your life."
- BISHOP TD JAKES

I CHOOSE TO BE ENCOURAGED

Isaiah 40:31, "But they that wait upon the Lord shall renew their strength; they shall mount up with wings as eagles; they shall run, and not be weary; and they shall walk, and not faint."

Psalm 121:1-2, "I lift up my eyes to the mountains where does my help come from? My help comes from the Lord, the Maker of heaven and earth."

It is so important for us to learn how to encourage ourselves in the midst of a storm. No matter what we are going though God can handle it. We have to stop waiting on others to encourage us, one of the greatest ways to encourage ourselves is the word of God. His desire is to up lift us when we are down. He tells us in 1 Peter 5:7 NLV Give all your worries and cares to God, for He cares for you. I believe that we can be confident that our help comes from God and that we can cast our care to Him, and He will take care of them. The important part is that we should be encouraged that He has the ability to love us through whatever we are going through. It is also important for us to share with others what God has done for us, which will encourage them to hold on because God has it all under control. I want you to choose to be encouraged.

How do you encourage yourself?

Do you depend on others or God to encourage you?

How can getting encouraged inspire you?

How does it help you grow?

Greatness awaits you! It is up to you to step into it!

Decide today that you will believe in the power that God has placed inside of you!

"Because what real fathers do is they make a deposit in you, through which you can make a withdrawal the rest of your life."
- BISHOP TD JAKES

I REFUSE TO GIVE THE DEVIL ANY VICTORY!

"The thief comes only in order to steal and kill and destroy. I have come that they may have and enjoy life, and have it in abundance to the fullest, till it overflows." John 10:10

The enemy loves when our men are not living up to their full potential! He does not want them to be the fathers they have been called to be. How does he carry out his mission? Through drugs, alcohol, abusive behavior, and sexual misconduct. The list goes on, but we serve a God who will come against the plans of the enemy! He comes to show us a life of joy and abundance and to teach and guide us down the pathway that he has for us to follow. He has given us the greatest manual of all times, His word!

When God is leading, we can be reassured that He is leading us to a life full of joy and abundance.

How have you given the enemy victory over your life?

Are you confident in God's power in your life?

Do you realize the enemy's assignment is to destroy you?

Greatness awaits you! It is up to you to step into it!

Decide today that you will believe in the power that God has placed inside of you!

"Because what real fathers do is they make a deposit in you, through which you can make a withdrawal the rest of your life."
- BISHOP TD JAKES

LEARNING HOW TO FORGIVE

Here, God is sharing the importance of forgiving.

Matthew 6:14-15: For if you forgive other people when they sin against you, your heavenly Father will also forgive you. But if you do not forgive others their sins, you Father will not forgive your sins.

When you stand praying, if you hold anything against anyone, forgive them. Mark 11:25 NIV

I love what the Word and Lewis Smedes have to say for you today about forgiveness.

When someone hurts us, our natural response is to either hurt them back or hope they will suffer for what they have done to us. Yet as redeemed children of God, we know this is the wrong response. That is when we discover forgiving someone doesn't come naturally or easily; it requires supernatural grace on our part. And where do we get that? Through prayer! Jesus said, "When you stand praying, if you hold anything against anyone, forgive them, so that your Father in Heaven may forgive you your sins." Recalling God's grace towards you leaves you no choice but to extend that same grace towards someone who hurts you.

Lewis Smedes said, "Forgiveness is a decision to set a prisoner free, and then discovering that the prisoner is you." So if you have a desire to forgive someone, get excited; the Holy Spirit has already done half the job. To complete the other half, humble yourself and pray: "Father, I turn from every desire I have to avenge this wrong. You saw the situation before it happened, and in Your infinite wisdom You allowed it to be so. Your Word says that 'all things work together for good' (Romans 8:28 KJV)—even this for my good—so from this moment on, with the help of Your Holy Spirit, I forgive them. I will not dwell on the situation but will declare Your word instead."

If you have someone that you have to forgive but are finding it hard to do, ask God to help you. I want to share with you a story about someone I had to forgive. I felt like I was a better friend to her than she was to me. What I found out was that she was jealous of me and my success.

Whenever we were together, I felt like she was always putting me down or trying to find something negative to say about me. I decided that it was time for me to end that so-called friendship. I heard something once: when you are in the presence of others, you should always leave feeling better than when you arrived. That was not the case with this person. After a while, I realized that I had to forgive her, but I did not have to stay connected with her!

I continued to pray for her and her family, and that helped me to feel better about forgiving her.

Are there people in your life you need to forgive?

What will forgiveness do for you?

Do you find it hard to forgive those who hurt you?

Greatness awaits you! It is up to you to step into it!

Decide today that you will believe in the power that God has placed inside of you!

"Because what real fathers do is they make a deposit in you, through which you can make a withdrawal the rest of your life."
- BISHOP TD JAKES

LEARN TO THINK STRATEGICALLY 1

I read this from the Word for you today.

So be careful how you live. Don't live like fools, but like those who are wise. Make the most of every opportunity in these evil days. Ephesians 5:15–16 NLT

Strategic thinking helps you to plan, to become more efficient, to maximize your strengths, and to find the most direct path towards achieving your God-given assignment in life. The benefits of strategic thinking are numerous. Here are a few of them:

(1) Strategic thinking simplifies the difficult. It takes complex issues and long-term objectives that can be very difficult to address and breaks them down into manageable sizes. Anything becomes simpler when you have a plan! The Bible says, "The plans of the diligent lead to profit as surely as haste leads to poverty." (Proverbs 21:5 NIV)

(2) Strategic thinking helps you to ask the right questions. Take a look at the following questions developed by Bobb Biehl, author of Master Planning. "Direction: What should we do next? Why? Organize: Who is responsible for what? Who is responsible for whom? Do we have the right people in the right places? Cash: What is our projected income, expense, net? Can we afford it? How can we afford it? Tracking: Are we on target? Overall evaluation: Are we achieving the quality we expect and demand of ourselves? Refinement: How can we be more effective and more efficient?"

These may not be the only questions you need to ask in order to begin formulating a strategic plan, but they are a good first step. Until you take the first step, you'll remain stuck. Until you get over your need to do it perfectly, you won't do it at all. You ask, "When should I start?" Today!

What plans do you have for your life?

Is your life in an uproar?

Are you one who thinks strategically?

Greatness awaits you! It is up to you to step into it!

Decide today that you will believe in the power that God has placed inside of you!

"Because what real fathers do is they make a deposit in you, through which you can make a withdrawal the rest of your life."
- BISHOP TD JAKES

LEARN TO THINK STRATEGICALLY 2

I read this from the Word for you today.

All who are prudent act with knowledge. Proverbs 13:16 NIV

By taking the time to acquire knowledge, you'll be ready for the opportunities life brings. If you are not prepared, they'll pass you by and go to others. God said, "My people are destroyed for lack of knowledge." (Hosea 4:6 KJV) Observe:

(1) Strategic thinking prepares you for the future. None of us know what tomorrow will bring. "Don't brag about your plans for tomorrow— wait and see what happens." (Proverbs 27:1 TLB) The only thing that's worse than the uncertainty of tomorrow is having no plan and strategy for your life.

(2) Strategic thinking reduces the margin of error. Whenever you shoot from the hip, you increase your margin of error. It's like a golfer stepping up to a ball and hitting it before lining up the shot. Misaligning a shot by a few degrees can send your ball a hundred meters off target. Strategic thinking lines up your actions with your objectives, just as lining up a shot in golf helps you to put the ball closer to the pin. The better you are aligned with your target, the better the odds that you will be going in the right direction.

(3) Strategic thinking gives you influence with others. One executive quipped, "Our company has a short-range plan and a long-range plan. Our short-range plan is to stay afloat long enough to make it to our long-range plan." That's hardly a strategy, yet it's the position some of us find ourselves in. The person with the plan is the one with the power. Whatever activity you're involved in, strategic thinking is essential to success. Talk to God about it.

Do you believe thinking strategically gives you influence with others?

How are you planning for your life that leaves no room for error?

Do you believe that planning helps you toward a great future?

Greatness awaits you! It is up to you to step into it!

Decide today that you will believe in the power that God has placed inside of you!

"Because what real fathers do is they make a deposit in you, through which you can make a withdrawal the rest of your life."
- BISHOP TD JAKES

LIFE WITH MY DAD

Psalm 103:13: The Lord is like a father to his children.

1 John 3:1: See what great love the Father has lavished on us, that we should be called children of God! And that is what we are!

Here are my thoughts:
A dad that will always listen and gives great advice.
He should never be afraid to show his feelings.
He is there to protect and guide his children.
He always shows his children how to keep their imagination flowing.
He doesn't have to be asked to be a father.
He doesn't have to be asked to spend time with his children; he just does what is natural to him.
Spending time with family brings him much joy.
He would never put anything before his family.
He will never have to be forced to care for his children.

Do you feel that having your father in your life made a big difference to you?

How would you sum up your dad's influence in your life?

What is your prospective of your dad and how he viewed his life as your father and provider?

Was you dad a loving kind of person?

Do you believe that it is the duty of a father to give his son a good chance?

Did your father believe in you and your dreams?

Greatness awaits you! It is up to you to step into it!

Decide today that you will believe in the power that God has placed inside of you!

"Because what real fathers do is they make a deposit in you, through which you can make a withdrawal the rest of your life."
- BISHOP TD JAKES

LIFE WITHOUT MY DAD

Most fathers live what they have learned.

Some men did not have Godly role models to follow.

There are those who did grow up with their father in the home, but he was not a good example for them to follow.

These men who did turn out okay, even though their father was not a great example. I believe that they decided to learn from their bad experience. They made up their minds to be a better father than the one who was set before them.

It is important that our young black males have role models in their lives.

When they cannot find the love they need they tend to turn to negative love, which to them says that any kind of love is better than no love.

It is important that we show our young black boys what is possible for them in life even if they do not have their fathers in their lives.

The bottom line is that we have the greatest Father of all, and that is our Father, Lord, and Savior, Jesus Christ.

When you think of your dad, how does it make you feel?

Would you change anything about how you grew up without your dad?

Did you ever make excuses because your dad was not there?

What does a perfect father look like to you?

Greatness awaits you! It is up to you to step into it!

Decide today that you will believe in the power that God has placed inside of you!

"Because what real fathers do is they make a deposit in you, through which you can make a withdrawal the rest of your life."
- BISHOP TD JAKES

LORD, GIVE ME YOUR WISDOM & KNOWLEDGE

2 Chronicles 1:10-12: That night, God appeared to Solomon and said to him, "Ask for whatever you want me to give you."

He replied, "Give me wisdom and knowledge, that I may lead this people, for who is able to govern this great people of yours?" Since you have not asked for long life, but for wisdom and knowledge to govern my people over whom I have made you king, therefore, wisdom and knowledge will be given you.

Wisdom vs. Knowledge, written by Royale Scuderi
Wisdom is the ability to discern and judge which aspects of that knowledge are true, right, lasting, and applicable to your life. It's the ability to apply that knowledge to the greater scheme of life. It's also deeper; knowing the meaning or reason; about knowing why something is, and what it means to your life.

Knowledge is the accumulation of facts and data that you have learned about or experienced. It's being aware of something and having information. Knowledge is really about facts and ideas that we acquire through study, research, investigation, observation, or experience.

Sadly, we can gain a lifetime of knowledge, yet never see the wisdom in it. We miss the deeper meaning of having wisdom.

I think that is was honorable that Solomon ask God for wisdom and knowledge. I believe in the beginning, it allowed him to make the right decisions pertaining to the people of God.

I really believe if we would spend more time seeking God for his wisdom and knowledge, we would live a healthier and prosperous life. That is what God desires for us.

I think it is important to seek God for his wisdom and knowledge to help you be better fathers. Whether you had your father in your life or not, this is the key to continually becoming a better father like our father Jesus Christ.

Do you think it is important to seek God's wisdom and knowledge?

If not, why?

Do you think if you would seek God for his wisdom and knowledge, it would help you to be a better father?

If not, why?

Greatness awaits you! It is up to you to step into it!

Decide today that you will believe in the power that God has placed inside of you!

"Because what real fathers do is they make a deposit in you, through which you can make a withdrawal the rest of your life."
- BISHOP TD JAKES

MY LOVE COVERS A MULTITUDE!

1 Peter 4:8 says, "Above all things, have an unfailing love for one another, for love covers a multitude of sins, forgives and disregards the offenses of others."

God is telling us that His love for us covers our sins, but we cannot continue committing the same sins over and over again and use the excuse that it is ok because God will forgive us, because God knows our hearts and our intentions. God's forgiveness does not justify our sins unless we sincerely repent and ask God for His strength and to help us overcome our weaknesses.

In 1 John 1:9, God tells us that if we confess our sins, He is faithful and just to forgive us our sins and cleanse us from all unrighteousness. However, there is a requirement: we must confess our sins. God wants us to know that He truly loves us and wants us to live the beautiful life that he created for us, but only if we are committed to following Him and allowing Him to direct us in His will. This reassures us that we are covered by His grace and mercy.

Are you sure that God has forgiven you?

Do you believe that God loves you despite your sins?

Do you believe that we please God when we do his will?

Do you need to confess any sins to the Lord?

Greatness awaits you! It is up to you to step into it!

Decide today that you will believe in the power that God has placed inside of you!

"Because what real fathers do is they make a deposit in you, through which you can make a withdrawal the rest of your life."
- BISHOP TD JAKES

RAISING BLACK MALES: KEY INGREDIENTS TO SUCCESSFUL OUTCOMES IN BLACK MALE DEVELOPMENT

This paper is based on a program presented at the 2012 American Counseling Association Conference, San Francisco, CA, March 21-25. Teandra V. Gordon, Richard C. Henriksen, Jr., and Mary Nichter

Gordon, Teandra V., is a Counselor in Education doctoral candidate at Sam Houston State University. She has experience as both an elementary school teacher and a marriage and family therapist, providing both counseling and parenting education to families in the Child Protective Services system. Her research interests include effective parenting practices, parenting education, and narrowing the achievement gap among ethnic minority students.

Henriksen, Jr., Richard C., is an associate professor at Sam Houston State University. He has experience as a community counselor with an emphasis on multicultural issues in counseling. His research interests include multicultural counseling, multiple heritage counseling, religious and spiritual issues in counseling, and counselor training.

Nichter, Mary, is a professor and coordinator of the Master's Program at Sam Houston State University. She has experience as a marriage and family therapist in private practice and hospital settings and experience as a school counselor at elementary and secondary levels. Her research interests include supervision, gatekeeping and non-academic disposition of beginning counseling students, and best practices for school counselors.

Historically, black males have had a unique experience in America that has not always been positive. However, today a black male is the President of the United States. Black males also hold positions as chief executive officers of corporations, attorneys, college professors, doctors, and other prominent and influential leaders in our society.

With all of the success gained by black men, who, in 2009, comprised approximately 12.6% of the U.S. population, they also account for approximately 39.4% of the prison and jail population (Nealy, 2008; U.S. Department of Justice, 2010). Additionally, black men continually have lower graduation rates and lower standardized test scores than their white counterparts (Stilwell, 2010). A research participant in a qualitative study by Maton, Hrabowski, and Greif (1998) encapsulated the unique experience of black men in America,

A white male...doesn't have to fight society's view of you. They're already saying, 'Oh well, you can be a doctor, you can be this.' But if you're a person of color, you have to prove [that you]...can excel, can be a doctor...it's sort of like you're assumed guilty, until proven innocent.

Due to the unique experience of black men in America and the variability of their outcomes, it is imperative for researchers to examine the key ingredients to successful outcomes in black male development. What is the role that parents, family, and society have in black male development, and what are the key influences that lead to successful outcomes?

Key Point: Researchers have continually found that parents have a powerful impact on child outcomes.

Theme 1: Fathers Are Role Models

Fathers were deemed as momentous influences in the lives of all of the participants. There were no criteria for having a relationship with their father, but each participant had a significant relationship with his father, and their fathers served as the most substantial influence on the men that they became. Even though each participant described his mother as doing most of the daily childrearing, when discussing what influenced the men that they became, they each discussed the things that they learned from their fathers. Significant to them were the things that their fathers told them, "[My father] would always preach on...how to conduct yourself," and how they watched their fathers live: "My dad wasn't a strong voice...he didn't really instill a lot into me verbally...but now when I look at it, it was his actions that were speaking louder than his words." Actions speak just as loud as words.

Theme 2: It Takes a Village!

The participants discussed the significant role that church, grandparents, and extended family had on their development. In going to church, a couple of participants learned about public speaking, "the involvement in the congregation played a huge role in my development...learning bible stories, scripture quoting...speaking at different events...that played a huge role in preparing me to do different things in the world," while others learned values that continued to guide them as men. Grandparents, aunts, and uncles were also a significant part of the young men's lives. "We had a lot of family around all the time. Just not my mom and dad, but their brothers and sisters were always around, so that had a lot of influence on me growing up." They remembered vacations, family gatherings, and Sunday dinners in which they were shaped by the influence of extended family members. The young men honored the role that their grandparents played in their lives. Three of the participants discussed the significant life lessons that they learned from their grandparents. One participant remarked, "My grandpa...he would be like...so y'all are learning about so and so [in school], well no it really happened like this..." Church and extended family members added richness, perspective, and additional role models into the lives of these developing black males.

Theme 3: Critical Juncture

A juncture is "a point of time, especially one made critical or important by a concurrence of circumstances" (juncture, n.d.). It is a point in time in which, "a decision must be made" (juncture, n.d.). The participants each described a time in their adolescence when they had to make a decision about the direction their lives would take. It was a time in their lives where they would either give in to negative peer pressure and experience the consequences that followed or overcome the imprudence of youth to make choices that would benefit their future. For some, this time involved experimenting with alcohol and drugs, and for others it involved criminal activity, or hanging around individuals who participated in criminal activity. This period aligns with Erikson's (1968) theory of psychosocial development. According to Erikson's theory, during the ages of 12 to 18 years old, a young man's development becomes independent of how he is treated by others, and is led by the decisions that he makes for himself. It is when a boy transitions to manhood and begins to determine his own sense of right and wrong and makes choices based on these convictions. During this transition, many young men make negative choices that lead to this critical juncture in which they will either continue to make those negative choices, or make choices that will benefit their future. One participant described his experience, "I think the thing that helped me was I knew where to go. A lot of times you have brothers that have the same issues that I have, they only know one place to go. Even if they want to go somewhere else...they have no idea...they are not familiar with...you know...I was getting in trouble but I was fresh off the dean's list in college." When living in a society where young black men heavily populate the criminal justice system, and juvenile pranks and follies committed by these young men are routinely considered criminal behavior, it is crucial that they are given the proper love, support, and guidance during this critical juncture in their development (Maton et al., 1998).

Theme 4: Exposure
The participants discussed the significant influence that being exposed to different experiences through extracurricular activities, family vacations, and parents' work environments had on their development. They were able to live beyond the routine environment of school and home and experience extracurricular activities such as sports and music lessons, some experienced trips across the country, and others experienced their parents in professional environments. These images and influences broadened their horizons and enlarged their vision for the future. They were able to stay busy with positive activity through extracurricular activities, experience other parts of the country and how other people lived through family vacations, and developed respect for their parents and a glimpse of what it is like to be a professional by visiting their parents' work environments. They credit this exposure with contributing to their future careers, life goals, and increasing their vision for what is possible for their own lives. One participant noted,
Growing up in [my neighborhood], if I would have stayed in [my neighborhood], if my parents wouldn't have taken me outside of [my neighborhood] and exposed me to other things, then I may have been caught up with the population there that may be comfortable with what is put in front of them...I think the exposure that I have received [really influenced me]. We got to get around other folks to see their way of

thinking and see their way of living. I think that [was] critical.

Theme 5: Education Was Mandatory
As adults, each of the men in our study valued the rewards of education. Though this value was developed in two different ways, half of the participants had parents, aunts, or uncles that graduated from college and success in school was not an option in their home. A sustained value was placed on education and their parents were very involved in their schooling from start to finish. These men grew up to value education as well, graduate from college, and choose various professional career paths. "My daddy instilled in us the value of education. It was one of those kind of homes, where you don't bring home below a B. He would always say, 'If you want to do well in life you have to get a good job, if you want to get a good job, you have to get a good education.'" The other half of the participants had parents who did not put a sustained focus on education, but instead valued the ethics of hard work and learning a trade. These men wished that their parents had stressed education and regretted not attending college. They developed a value for education in their own life experiences and hope to pass this value on to their children,

They never really stressed education. It was never really stressed. It was more experiential...where you get experience through life...nobody really talked about doing your homework, getting good grades. I wish somebody would have stressed education because I think I had the smarts to be further along in life. I'm trying to do it now because I understand, but had I had that person there to nurture then I could have been a lot further than I am today.

Theme 6: Essential Ingredients
The last theme emerged from the question, "Based on your own experience, knowledge, and insight; what do you believe it takes to raise a successful Black male in America today?" The essential ingredients that emerged from this question stemmed from the previous themes including: fathers as role models, extended family support, church, exposure, extracurricular activities, and a sustained emphasis on education. An additional factor that was added was the theme of Friendship. The participants recalled a strong authoritative relationship

with their fathers, and they wished that they would have felt comfortable talking to them about the many issues those young men faced as they grew up. The participants desire a friendship with their sons, one in which their sons would feel comfortable talking to them about anything. They valued the parental role, but Randall, a participant summed it up by saying,

I want to [be] their friend, but their parent at the same time. Some people say that you can't do both, but I don't believe that. I think you can be a parent and a friend. I think in certain situations you have to choose one, but I think you can do it in a way that you still show yourself friendly.

Implications for Counselors and Family Therapists
Counselors and family therapists can play a significant role in educating parents regarding the themes that have emerged from this research. Most parents love their children and want what is best for them. Without knowledge of the essential ingredients to healthy development, they are unable to implement these ingredients in their son's lives. Counselors and family therapists can educate parents regarding the important role that fathers play in their developing sons' lives. Divorcing parents need to be especially made aware of the significance of maintaining and nurturing the father-son relationship. Fathers are the main role model in their son's lives and if a father is not present, it is important for grandparents, extended family members, church personnel, coaches, and other male role models to purposely make an impact in the lives of these young men. They are watching for someone to emulate.

Parents and teachers should be educated about the critical juncture that young men experience. It is important that these young men are not eternally condemned for bad choices; this is a time for learning, growth, and second chances. Counselors and therapists should be sensitive to this critical juncture and advocate against injustices that may occur in the school system or criminal justice system regarding racial inequality that affects the consequences for poor choices. It is imperative that young men are given the opportunity to overcome foolish youthful actions and make choices that can benefit their futures.

Counselors and family therapists should educate parents and schools about the importance of exposing young black men to various activities and experiences. As young people are exposed to different places and people, they are able to discover their own interests and passions. Developing a passion for something early in life where talent and time can be dedicated to creating a future is a huge protector against negative outcomes in young black men.

Parents also need to be educated regarding the significance of parental roles and college. This value must be established early in life and sustained throughout their development (Herndon & Moore, 2002). It is important for parents to value education and let both their words and actions reflect this value. This strongly increases the likelihood that this value will be passed on to their children.

What did you get most out of reading this article?

Why do you think it is so hard for the black family to realize the importance of professional counseling?

Based on your prospective, what do you think it takes to raise a successful black male?

How important is it to expose our children to different cultures and things of the world?

How important is it to look towards the future and not look at where you may be right now?

Do you believe that it takes a village to raise a child and if so, why?

Greatness awaits you! It is up to you to step into it!

Decide today that you will believe in the power that God has placed inside of you!

"Because what real fathers do is they make a deposit in you, through which you can make a withdrawal the rest of your life."
- BISHOP TD JAKES

THE TAPESTRY OF LOVE

I read this from the NRSV Daily Bible (I added a few thoughts).

One friend may offer us affection. Another may simulate our minds. Another may strengthen our souls. The more we are able to receive the different gifts our friends have to give us, the more we are able to offer our own unique but limited gifts. I believe that the friendship of a father creates a beautiful tapestry of true love. I believe that our black men need just that - a tapestry of true fatherly friendship that causes them to support each other's gifts. I really believe when that happens, they are able to see the true value of the friendship of a father. That allows them to trust in their own gifts no matter what happened to them in life. It instills in them that they are powerful, talented, and loving. What I know for sure is they have been created with greatness from Almighty God.

As a black man, what are your fears about building a friendship?

Do you believe that you have been created with greatness in you?

How do you deal with all the racism this country has brought upon you?

What is your best advice to young black boys and young black men growing up in a world that is so filled with racism?

Greatness awaits you! It is up to you to step into it!

Decide today that you will believe in the power inside of you!

"Because what real fathers do is they make a deposit in you, through which you can make a withdrawal the rest of your life."
- BISHOP TD JAKES

THE TRUE LOVE OF A FATHER

1 John 4:7: Anyone who does not love does not know God. God is love. Whoever lives in love lives in God, and God in him.

Jeremiah 31:3: Long ago the Lord said to Israel: "I have loved you, my people, with an everlasting love. With unfailing love, I have drawn you to myself."

The true love of God shows us how important it is to follow the example of our Father's heavenly love. The fact that he loves us unconditionally is the key to true love. No matter what we do, He is always there to forgive us. Time heals all wounds, and healing allows love in. The love of our earthly father is important to us; however, there is nothing like the love of our Heavenly Father, and God created us to love one another as He loves us!

He is the greatest reflection of love. He is love, and since God is perfect and we are not, it makes us the perfect recipients of His love. True love keeps no record of wrong. It is not rude, it is not selfish, and it is not evil. It is kind and giving.

True love brings us joy! It makes you want to be your best self. So, the next time those feelings about your father cross your mind, ask God to help you to love him as He loves you both.

How do you feel about the love of your father or the lack thereof?

Have you moved on from those negative feelings about your father?

Do you find it hard to love him unconditionally?

Greatness awaits you! It is up to you to step into it!

Decide today that you will believe in the power that God has placed inside of you!

"Because what real fathers do is they make a deposit in you, through which you can make a withdrawal the rest of your life."
- BISHOP TD JAKES

THE TRUTH WILL SET YOU FREE

John 8:31-32: So Jesus said to those Jews who had believed in Him, "If you abide in My word, hold fast to My teachings, and live in accordance with them, you are truly My disciples. And you will know the Truth, and the Truth will set you free."

I really believe that when we are able to face the truth head on, it can set us free. The worst thing in the world is to lie to yourself and refuse to acknowledge the truth about the things we need to change in our lives. Our failures should show us the things we need to change, and that can only happen when we are open to receive the truth about what it is that we need to change. When I need to change something about myself, I ask God to show me what I need to change. Doing this is helping me to grow and mature. It helps me learn from my mistakes so that I can be who I have been destined to be in Christ Jesus.

William Shakespeare said, "To thine own self be true, and it must follow, as night the day, that thou canst not then be false to any man."

"I am the Way, the Truth, and the life." Jesus Christ

"The truth is rarely pure and is never simple."

Take time and think about the truth about yourself that you need to deal with! And always keep it real!

What do you need to be honest with yourself about?

How does it make you feel when you tell the truth?

How does it make you feel when you don't tell the truth?

Greatness awaits you! It is up to you to step into it!

Decide today that you will believe in the power that God has placed inside of you!

"Because what real fathers do is they make a deposit in you, through which you can make a withdrawal the rest of your life."
- BISHOP TD JAKES

THERE IS NO CLASS THAT TEACHES YOU HOW TO BE A GOOD FATHER

There is no class that teaches a man how to be a good father. However, there is a manual that instructs and guides him on how to become the father God intended for him to be. That manual is called the Bible. Let's take a look at what God says about fatherhood in His Bible.

Proverbs 22:6: Train up a child in the way they should go, and when they grow up, they will not depart from it.

I believe the best way to follow this scripture is to show your children love and kindness You should also spend quality time with them, building wonderful memories with them. Teach them to always be honest and to respect and treat others the way they want to be treated. When they grow up, they will remember what you have taught them.

Ephesians 6:4: Fathers, do not irritate and provoke your children to anger and do not exasperate them to resentment, but rear them tenderly in the training and discipline and the counsel and admonition of the Lord.

It is important that we discipline our children in love and compassion. We never want our children to show resentment toward us. I believe that all children want from their fathers is love. Don't spend too much time focusing on what they are doing wrong. Instead, focus on what they are doing right. When you do have to discipline them, do so in love so they will know how much you care. It is important that they know there is nothing they can do that can stop you from loving them.

2 Corinthians 3:2: You yourselves are our letter of recommendation (our credentials), written in your hearts, to be known and read by everybody.

This says that your children are always watching you. As they watch, make sure you give them something good to see. This scripture teaches who we are and how we should live in Christ. This is a letter from God showing you the way we should act.

Deuteronomy 6:4-6: Love the Lord our God, the Lord is one. Love the Lord your God with all your heart and with all your soul and with all your strength. Impress them on your children, talk about them when you sit at home and when you walk along the road, when you lie down and when you get up.

This is why we should spend quality time with our children - so they can see the real us. God wants us to keep love in our hearts. Being a great father does not mean that you are perfect! We all make mistakes, and it is good for our children to see us fall and how we handle it by getting back up and starting the race all over again.

That is what God does. He loves us unconditionally no matter how many times we fall. He is still there with open arms to embrace us.

Psalm115:14-15: May the Lord give you increase more and more you and your children. May you be blessed by the Lord, who made heaven and earth.

There is nothing more powerful than to see the love of a father for his children—his ability to create a loving and safe environment for his children. He is not afraid to commit his matters to God in prayer and then take action. Children are more eager to follow in their fathers' footsteps when they see him roll up his sleeves and set the pace for them to follow. That is why it is so important for us to lead by example with our children. If we raise our children by the golden rule, they are bound to do the right thing. Children are like a precious stone that shines brightly, but they will only shine if we take care of them.

How was your relationship with your dad? Was it good or bad?

Do you look to the Bible for help with your children?

How do you lead your children by example?

Greatness awaits you! It is up to you to step into it!

Decide today that you will believe in the power that God has placed inside of you!

"Because what real fathers do is they make a deposit in you, through which you can make a withdrawal the rest of your life."
- BISHOP TD JAKES

*"Any man can be a father; it takes a
special person to be a dad!"*
- UNKNOWN AUTHOR

*"Father is the noblest title a man can be given. It is more
than a biological role. It signifies a patriarch, a leader, an
exemplar, a confidant, a teacher, a hero, and a friend."*
- ROBERT L. BLACKMAN

*"One thing that prevents a man from being a good
father is he hasn't completed being a boy."*
- IYANLA VANZANT

*"Fathers see the greatness in their children, and they
keep them close to protect who they will become."*
- NORA SHARIFF BORDEN

*"The greatest gift a father can give a child is to love
them for who they are and who they will become!"*
- NORA SHARIFF BORDEN

*"Blessed indeed is the man who hears many
gentle voices—call him father!"*
- LYDIA M. CHILD

*"Dads hold our hands for a little while and
hold our hearts forever!"*
- UNKNOWN AUTHOR

*"The way your skin sparkles in the light is the
way God created you to be."*
- AMARIAH HASSAN

UNCONDITIONAL LOVE NEVER FAILS

1 Corinthians 13:4-8: Love is patient, love is kind. It does not envy, it does not boast, it is not proud. It does not dishonor others, it is not self-seeking, it is not easily angered, it keeps no record of wrongs. Love does not delight in evil but rejoices with the truth. It always protects, always trusts, always hopes, always perseveres. Love never fails.

How do you love a parent who left you? This is a hard one. I learned to love unconditionally, but my sister found it very difficult, so she decided to close her heart to our father. I guess I saw the good he could be, his potential, and not who he actually was, which was a drug addict. I felt the pain, but I just learned how to deal with it - all the unkept promises, not being there for me when I needed him the most. Even now as I write, the tears are filling up in my eyes. One thing I was sure of was that hating him would not make me feel any better, so I had to love him and accept him for who he was, just like Christ does for us! I'm sure God's heart hurts when we don't live up to our full potential. I really do understand how the men featured in this book feel about not having their fathers in their lives. I know how easy it was to turn to gangs, drugs and the street life to try to make themselves feel better.

I am sure they felt that any kind of love was better than no love at all, but only because they didn't know that there is a greater love, and that is the love of our true Father, Jesus Christ! His love will never fail us, it will always comfort us in our times of need, and I know that if we were to think back over our lives, we would see the footprints of God carrying us through all the pain and loss of those we wish loved us.

I truly believe that the Lord wants us to know how much He really does love and care for us. It's never too late to turn to Him for help!

So, as you are reading this, please take the time to forgive your father for the pain he may have caused you!

Decide to love him unconditionally, just as Christ loves us.

True unconditional love never fails!

Are you finding it hard to forgive your father?

How do you deal with those feelings?

If your father is still living, are you willing to forgive him?

Who do you seek for help through your pain?

Greatness awaits you! It is up to you to step into it!

Decide today that you will believe in the power that God has placed inside of you!

"Because what real fathers do is they make a deposit in you, through which you can make a withdrawal the rest of your life."
- BISHOP TD JAKES

WHAT'S WRONG WITH ME?

Nina Keegan said it best!

The Lord repeatedly tells us in His Word that He is the great "I AM." I always wondered why He never added anything else to that statement. I felt like God was being vague and leaving out all the important details and awe-inspiring adjectives He could have used to enhance His own resume or curriculum vitae. Yet, He chose not to.

At no better time do the words "less is more" or "simple abundance" hold more truth! God's unvarnished, powerfully simplistic, two small words say more about our most awesome God than a whole novel ever could! They assure us that no traits defining God could ever be left out. "I AM" says it all. The magnitude of that is amazing! He Just Is!

I love this because the next time you ask, What's wrong with me?" Just know what the great I Am thinks of you and what He chooses to say about you. We are made in His likeness and image, proving that there is nothing wrong with you, but everything right with you because of who you are in Christ! I read this quote by August Strindberg the other day, "There are poisons that blind you and poisons that open your eyes." I want you to look at the poisons in your life as an eye opener! Say this to yourself every morning and night before you go to bed:

"I am powerful. I am great. I am made in the image of God."

Do you believe that there is something wrong with you?

If so, how do you deal with that?

What is your focus on who you are?

Greatness awaits you! It is up to you to step into it!

Decide today that you will believe in the power that God has placed inside of you!

"Because what real fathers do is they make a deposit in you, through which you can make a withdrawal the rest of your life."
- BISHOP TD JAKES

"There is nothing wrong with me because I have been created in the image of the one who only creates beautiful things."
- NORA SHARIFF BORDEN

"Your positive actions, combined with your positive thinking, results in success."
- SHIV KHERA

"Whatever we think about ourselves will come to pass if we keep thinking and speaking it!"
- NORA SHARIFF BORDEN

"Decided that each day you will open your mind to receive all that God has for you."
- NORA SHARIFF BORDEN

"I am in total charge of my life because God says so!"
- NORA SHARIFF BORDEN

"The Holy Spirit that gave me the desires of my heart leads, guides, and reveals to me the perfect plan that He has for my life."
- DR. GEORGE D HAMILTON

WELL-KNOWN
BLACK MEN

MARTIN DELANY

Martin Delany was a man who made a habit of defying the odds. He was self-educated in a time when, for blacks, being educated could mean death. He was a physician, author, business owner and military pioneer at a time when African Americans were still counted as chattel and their intelligence doubted.

Born a free black man in 1812 in what was then Charlestown, Va., (now Charles Town, W. Va.) Delany learned to read by eavesdropping outside the classroom of his white friends.

Barred from learning in his early years, Delany later became one of the first blacks to be admitted to Harvard Medical School, where he was not permitted to continue due to the objections of the white students who resented being in a classroom with a negro

In addition to a career in medicine, Delany also owned a newspaper. But he also distinguished himself as a racial activist. An African-American abolitionist, Delany buttressed

"We want African Americans to remember the hardships and struggle of those who came before us that had to endure and overcome in order for us as a race of people to be where we are today," Roper said of the commemoration.

Delany was a recruiter for several U.S. Colored Troops (USCT) regiments including the 54th Massachusetts Infantry Volunteers. He was later commissioned a major, becoming the first Black line officer in the U. S. Army. He died in 1885.

DANIEL HALE WILLIAMS

Daniel Hale Williams, (born January 18, 1858, Hollidaysburg, Pennsylvania, U.S.—died August 4, 1931, Idlewild, Michigan), American physician and founder of Provident Hospital in Chicago, credited with the first successful heart surgery.

Williams graduated from Chicago Medical College in 1883. He served as surgeon for the South Side Dispensary (1884–92) and physician for the Protestant Orphan Asylum (1884–93). In response to the lack of opportunity for African Americans in the medical professions, he founded (1891) the country's first interracial hospital, Provident. In addition to offering medical care to African American patients, Provident provided training for African American interns and ran the first school for African American nurses in the United States. Williams was a surgeon at Provident (1892–93, 1898–1912) and surgeon in chief of Freedmen's Hospital, Washington, D.C. (1894–98), where he established another school for African American nurses.

It was at Provident Hospital that Williams performed daring heart surgery on July 10, 1893. Although contemporary medical opinion disapproved of surgical treatment of heart wounds, Williams opened the patient's thoracic cavity without aid of blood transfusions or modern anesthetics and antibiotics. During the surgery he examined the heart, sutured a wound of the pericardium (the sac surrounding the heart), and closed the chest. The patient lived at least 20 years following the surgery. Williams's procedure is cited as the first recorded repair of the pericardium; some sources, however, cite a similar operation performed by H.C. Dalton of St. Louis in 1891.

JESSE L. BROWN

Jesse L. Brown: the son of a sharecropper who became a Navy hero.

Jesse LeRoy Brown was born October 13th 1916 into very modest circumstances. Born 5 months after Bessie Coleman's last flight, Brown was raised in different parts of Mississippi, depending on where his father secured employment. Brown was a determined young person, and he excelled in his schoolwork, graduating from his high school with honors. The flying bug caught him early; at the age of six, his father took him to an air show, and it determined the course of his life. He read about aviation constantly and learned that black pilots did indeed exist (one of the pilots he learned about was Bessie Coleman). At that point, no African American pilots had yet been admitted to the U.S. military, and the brash young Brown even wrote a letter to President Franklin D. Roosevelt to question this state of affairs.

Brown applied to an integrated college, Ohio State, and supported himself in his studies by working several part-time jobs. In 1945, he learned that the U.S. Navy was recruiting pilots, and he applied. Despite meeting resistance because of his race, Brown was admitted to the program because his entrance exams were of such high quality. In 1947, he completed three phases of naval officer training in Illinois, Iowa, and Florida, including advanced flight training. Soon he was skilled at flying fighter aircraft, and in 1948, he received his Naval Aviator Badge. He received his navy commission and became an officer in 1949. The newspapers paid attention to Brown's progress, and his status as a commissioned naval officer made him a symbol of black achievement in black and white publications alike (he would be profiled in both The Chicago Defender and Life)

In the summer of 1950, the Korean War broke out, and Brown's ship, the carrier USS Leyte, was sent to the Korean peninsula. Brown and his fellow pilots flew daily missions to protect troops threatened by China's entrance into the war that November. On December 4th, flying with his squadron of six planes over enemy targets, Brown discovered that he was losing fuel, probably the result of Chinese infantry fire. He crashed and landed his plane and survived the crash, but his leg was pinned under the debris of his plane and he could not free it. Brown's wingman Thomas J Hudner, the pilot closest to him in the air, spotted Brown and took the unusual step of crash landing his own aircraft to try to save him. However, Brown had lost a lot of blood and was already falling in and out of consciousness. An attempt to bring in a helicopter failed as night fell, and by the morning it was undeniable that Brown was dead. Although Brown died young, his story would inspire many African-Americans to become military pilots. Furthermore, the dedication evinced by Hudner, a white man, for his squadron leader in the heat of war proved just how irrelevant matters of race could be in the military, which had so often been a historically volatile arena for race relations. Hundner said "I had no qualms about becoming friends with a man of a different color," "From an early age, my father had taught me: 'A man will reveal his character through his actions, not his skin color.'"

WILLIAM H. HASTIE

William H. Hastie: Lawyer and Judge

William Hastie was born in Knoxville, Tennessee in 1904, and like Coleman or Brown, he showed precocious intelligence and an early determination to succeed. His parents, a government clerk and a teacher, were in a better position than most to help their son excel, and he attended Amherst College in Massachusetts, where he graduated at the top of his class. Inspired by his cousin Charles Houston, who had a position at the Howard University School of Law, Hastie decided to enroll in law school. After an exceptional academic career, he passed the bar exam and became a practicing lawyer and a teacher at Howard. In 1933, he returned to Harvard to obtain his doctorate in judicial studies. It was at this point that the new administration of President Roosevelt took notice of the young man, who now called Washington, D.C. his home. He was one of the first African Americans appointed by the administration, serving as a lawyer with the Department of the Interior. As part of his work there, he drafted a constitution for the Virgin Islands, which had become an American territory after World War I. Taking note of his work, Roosevelt appointed Hastie to the federal court in the Virgin Islands, effectively making him the first federal African-American judge in history. He wouldn't stay very long, however, because of the outbreak of World War II – Hastie left for a job in the War Department, where he hoped to promote the integration of training units. Unfortunately, his attempts to do so were frustrated, and the idea would not take hold until after he had moved on. Hastie's outspokenness, however, had much to do with spurring public debate on the subject.

Hastie returned to the Virgin Islands when Congress passed an act assigning a governor to the region, which until that point had been loosely governed by the Department of the Interior and the military. Roosevelt appointed Hastie to be that first governor, making him the very first black governor of a U.S. state or territory to serve a full term (back in 1872, Pinckney Pinchback had served 35 days when the governor of Louisiana was impeached, making him technically the first African American governor in history, but his service was a stopgap measure). Hastie's first love remained the law, however, and he returned to the mainland in 1949 to accept President Harry Truman's nomination of him to the federal court of appeals. Although there was resistance to his nomination in the Senate, which took six months to confirm him, Truman's support carried the day and Hastie became a federal judge in 1950. He would hold the position until his retirement in 1971.

As the highest-ranking black federal judge, Hastie was able to speak openly about racism and segregation and support decisions that combatted them. Of course, he also addressed innumerable cases that had nothing to do with race, and he became one of the most respected members of the bench. It seemed likely for a time that he would be nominated for the Supreme Court, but although this nomination never came to pass (Thurgood Marshall would become the first black Supreme Court justice in 1967), Hastie left behind a record of public service that few could better. After retirement, Hastie became an activist for black causes and a lawyer for public interest groups until his death in 1976.

These powerful, well-known black men, who came from different backgrounds, yet seemed to be remarkably similar, were hard workers. I want to even go as far as to say visionaries. Although they had obstacles in their lives, they did not allow them to stop them from going after their dreams. I love the fact that they seemed to be determined and relentless to be successful. It breaks my heart that they had to go through so much just to live a life that had been promised to them by God himself! All because of the color of their skin.

FROM A
BLACK MAN'S
PERSPECTIVE

CLYDE MORGAN

Nora's father, Clyde Morgan, was a former U.S. Army Veteran. He was also a great, gifted artist who could carve anything out of a piece of wood. He leaves behind a legacy as the father of five children, ten grandchildren, and 27 great-grandchildren.

COUNTLESS CONVERSATIONS ABOUT CLYDE MORGAN

My husband and I have had countless conversations about the men in our lives (family and friends) that we knew who did not grow up with their fathers in their lives and how it affected them in life.

These conversations made me think about my father, Clyde Morgan, and how he enlisted in the army at a young age and when he returned home, he was addicted to heroin—a habit that he found too hard to quit. He was in so much pain emotionally from both the trauma of the army, as well as the effects of his father's absence, that he couldn't let the drugs go. I believe that his inability to be the father that we needed as children, was due to the fact that his father was not there for him. The drugs became a substitute for the love he so desperately needed from his father. My grandmother, his mother, was a loving and kindhearted woman who loved him so much she was unable to give him the tuff love that he so needed.

I heard something from one of my best friends that really grab hold of my heart and reminded me of my grandmother. She asked her grandmother how could she keep helping her father and her 102 year old grandmother said to her, your children are always on you, when they're no longer on your lap they are always on your heart! She said when you have children of your own you will know what I mean! I really believe this is how my grandmother felt about my father. I really believe that our black men must realize that when their father is not present that it is important for them to step up and be the father they were meant to be. They may not be perfect but perfect is not what they are called to be. They are called to be the best they can be, and God will supply the rest! Unfortunately, my father never understood the greatness that God placed inside of him and so he died taking his greatness to the grave with him. Decide you will not take your greatness to the grave with you!

What are you dealing with that keeps you from walking in your greatness?

Are you able to forgive your father for not being there?

How are you working on being the best you can be?

Are you dealing with any emotional pain?

Greatness awaits you! It is up to you to step into it!

Decide today that you will believe in the power that God has placed inside of you!

"Because what real fathers do is they make a deposit in you, through which you can make a withdrawal the rest of your life."
- BISHOP TD JAKES

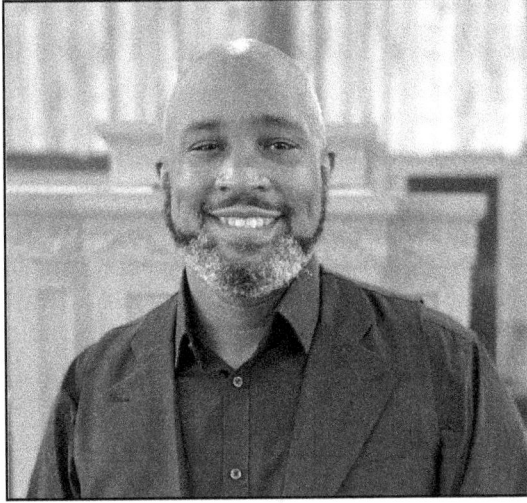

PASTOR KEITH BARNWELL

Keith A. Barnwell is a native of Cleveland, Ohio and is married to Robyn Barnwell. They share three daughters and one grandson. Keith earned an Associate Degree from Liberty University where he majored in Biblical Studies. He has been an entrepreneur for 15 years. He is the third generation Pastor of the Lily Baptist Church, located in Cleveland, Ohio.

THREE GENERATIONS OF PASTORS

My relationship and time spent with my dad growing up has always been consistent. Even though he worked many crazy hours and shifts, it never got in the way of him and me spending time together. Whether it was doing yard work, going on bike rides for hours, eating ice cream, or even going to his friend's house just to hang out, I was his little shadow! Wherever he went, it was almost a given that I wanted to go, too. Having my father at home allowed me to see things such as hard work and doing whatever was necessary to take care of the family. I am who I am because of my dad! My life is a total of everything he exposed me to. He drove a truck for a living, and now I drive a truck for a living. He was in management; I was also in management. He was a Pastor, and now I'm a Pastor. The list goes on and on.

The dad that I have is the same type of dad he had. My father saw his parents stay married for sixty-plus years, and my parents are celebrating fifty-plus years. His influence also spills over into my marriage, because I saw with my very own eyes how to fight to keep a marriage alive and how it's possible to have longevity in it as well. I know how it made me feel to see my dad every day. It gave me a sense of security to know that I had someone there who was masculine in every way, but also knew how to show that he cared by going to the grocery store together or cooking meals to the best of his ability. This in turn created this love for me to do the same for my wife and kids.

If there is anything that I wish could have been different growing up, it would be that he could have made it to more of my games in high school. It wasn't a lack of willingness to be there; it was because of his work schedule. Speaking of sports, that's the one thing that we never had in common. He was never into sports, but I absolutely love them to this day. I feel totally fulfilled as a man because he affirmed me as a child, encouraged me as a teen, and continued to teach me all the way into adulthood. I could go into the whole story of being the "Third Generational Pastor" of the same church, but that may just have to wait for the second book.

There are so many things that I can say about my father and this particular subject that this may just encourage me to write my very own book. Thank you for your vision and passion to get these types of stories available for others to read.

ANTHONY CLEMENTS

Anthony Clements is currently the Senior Director of Making Wealth Real Financial (MWR). He is a passionate educator of music and success principles of life. Also, he is the author of "ClemNotes for Teachers and Speakers" due to be released later this year.

TAUGHT BEFORE IT WAS CAUGHT

My relationship with my father was pretty good throughout my life. When I was a toddler, my perspective of him was defined by fun and fear. He and I used to watch professional wrestling, screaming at the television to our favorite guy Tommy Wildfire Rich. We cheered and booed at the television screen! Afterwards, we'd wrestle on the floor, and he would let me pin him down for three counts for the World Championship belt!

Even with all the fun, my dad was a strong disciplinarian, and that's when I feared him. When it came to me being obedient, he was strict. I wasn't a "bad" kid, just a little mischievous at times like most little boys. I remember when he bought me a green inchworm to ride on for Christmas. He put a yellow hard hat on its head, and he warned me not to ride it outside of the yard. I was having so much fun on it that I completely forgot what my dad said. Before I knew it, I was out of the yard, and when he saw me, he stared at me with those eyes. Whenever I saw him with those eyes, I knew I was in trouble! As I got older, he began to apologize for all the times when he was too strict.

It made me feel good having my father at home. His presence was a strong indication that everything was alright!

If anything needed fixing, my daddy could either fix it or mess it up further. It was hilarious how he never wanted to read the instructions. He always said, "I don't need no paper. I got God!" He said that with so much passion and conviction because he was a Baptist preacher. One time, he was trying to fix the fuse box with a screwdriver and a nail. As he stuck the nail in the box he exclaimed, "In the name of Jesus!" Fire started shooting out of the box and burned his face. He was hairless, which made him hard to look at, especially since I was used to seeing him heavily bearded. Now he looked like a shaved bird!

He was no professional, but he refused to sit around and let things in our house go unfixed. He would rather put forth the effort in being our family's handyman, even if he didn't know what he was doing. His presence was strong in our home. He was a natural born comedian who kept the family happy with laughter. When things went wrong, he went outside and prayed about it. He didn't let me go with him, as if he didn't want me to see the man behind the curtain like in the

Wizard of Oz. I consider myself blessed to physically have him in my life. He stayed when things were good, and he especially stayed when things got hard, as they often did. He wasn't perfect, but he was a great example of a man who was committed to his family. Like many families, we appeared happy and holy on the outside, but behind closed doors we were like any normal family, with arguments and disagreements. Although my dad was a preacher, he cussed like a sailor at home.

My dad wasn't the one that sat me down and taught me all the things a fathers should teach his son, like how to fix things, how to change a tire, how to keep a job, or how to be happily married. My granddad, Big Daddy, taught me those things. However, my dad did support me - as well as the family - as a whole. I am who I am because of what my dad and my grandfather showed me, but also because of things that I chose to do once I got older, like read books on life to understand how it all works. I also reached out to many father figures to help guide me and pour into me as I grew and matured.

The foundation that my dad set for me to rear my children was that of being present, both at home and in their lives. I understand that my presence is a gift. My dad was there for all of my graduations, as am I with my children. His gift of attention encouraged my gift of music and speech, and I am depositing those qualities into my children. His gift of providing and protection kept us moving to different phases in our lives. The balancing act of discipline and laughter are definitely in the fabric of my parental style! God did not call us to be perfect, but to be FAITHFUL! I learned those strong, foundational practices by observation, and I implement them as I rear my children.

I will always remember the time I was the star actor in a play. After I said my lines, his voice cut through the silence of the audience and screamed, "ALLLL RIGHT, BOY!" He wanted so badly to get me onto the famous show "Star Search" with Ed McMahan, but he didn't have the money to pay entrance fees. The fact that he believed in me enough to have those dreams for me was good enough for me.

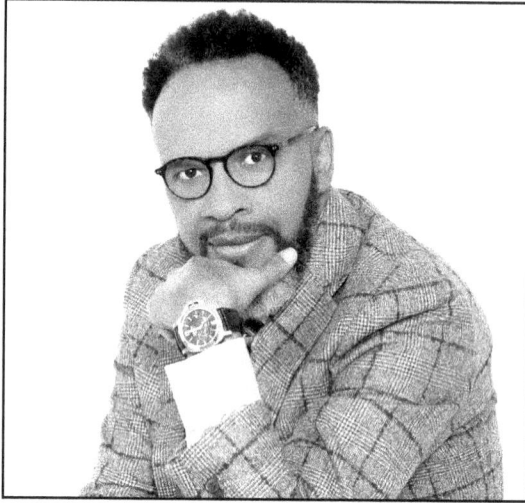

DR. ANTHONY EARL

Dr. Anthony Earl is known as one given to details and possesses exceptional biblical insight. He is driven by a mandate to equip and encourage leaders to return to the authentic biblical patterns given by God. Anthony has Bachelor of Arts, Master of Divinity, and Doctorate of Ministry degree from Wilberforce University and Garrett Evangelical Seminary on the campus of Northwestern University. He pastored for 30 years and now travels extensively serving as a mentor to leaders both nationally and internationally. Anthony lives in Chicago, Illinois, and Brentwood, California with his wife, Caterina. He has five adult children and is a proud grandfather.

MY AMAZING FATHER

I am a blessed man who had an amazing father. Mr. Robert Earl, Sr. provided a very safe environment, great resources, and a wealth of wisdom to our family. I am who I am today because of the great example my father set for me and because of what he modeled in our home when I was younger. When I look through the lens of my own personal journey with my dad, I am uplifted and refreshed.

I watched him manage his money skillfully and bring it home to my mother, who managed the household finances. They worked seamlessly in their partnership, and it provided a great example for my siblings and me. His generous benevolence influenced me greatly, and I attribute a lot of my personality to him. His kind heart, commitment, and loyalty are certainly some of the characteristics that influenced my life. My siblings and I also have those same traits. Every child deserves to be loved and fathered like my dad did for us. It's parenting at its finest.

Dad volunteered often to help in the community. Whether it was a school activity or assisting a neighbor, he was there at their beck and call, another trait that was passed down to me. Since I was a young man, I have always volunteered to help others in need. It is still a principle that is prevalent in my life today, and it's how I operate in my ministry. My dad wasn't perfect man, but he was good.

He lost his mother at the age of three and was practically raised by his oldest sister, my Aunt Josephine. His father, my Grandpa Hugh, was born in the early 1900s. He was a strict, hard-working minister. In my dad's early twenties, he was young and single, living in urban Chicago. He overcame many challenges and did well for himself.

He learned how to be a better father over time. There is no class that teaches us how to be good fathers. If there was, I wonder how many mistakes would have been avoided. Many learn from their mistakes and stop their children from repeating those same mistakes, and some barely succeed in raising their children because of the lack of good examples in their lives to teach them. I am so grateful to have had a father who was such a great example and who is so deserving of the honor due to him.

If someone like my dad was able to do a good job raising his children with very little help, I can only imagine how much better off we would be as African American families with more examples of exceptional fathers. There is nothing like the support of a father, even when you make mistakes.

Dad's wisdom and support helped me to change the destructive habits and lifestyle I was creating for myself. He taught me the importance of taking control of my destiny, and he taught me with passion. Our relationship had some major challenges, but we overcame them together with hard work.

Our home was filled with love and lots of laughter and joy. We were one of the few black families that had a father in the home and who went on family vacations together.

Unfortunately, as I grew older, our relationship weakened. I chose to live differently, and it created a very tense environment. Thankfully, mom was there to intervene and mediate on my behalf. However, my reverence for my dad often kept me from making choices that could have been harmful or even deadly for me. The very thought of him would stop me in my tracks. That is the true influence of a good father! I always desired a close relationship with my father, and I worked at making it a reality, just as he did. The poor choices I made as a kid didn't stop him from finding ways to connect with me and enhance our father and son bond. My involvement with gangs, drugs, and street life put our relationship to the test, but with the help of my mom, he consistently and continuously looked for ways to steer me down the right path. Despite all of my rebellious behavior as an adolescent, he was always there, helping me through those times.

I am also grateful that my father had good friends who made a positive impression on me. They were great role models. It is a blessing to have had other good male figures that stepped in to help my dad point me in the right direction. He had a best friend since grade school who I have always called Uncle Johnnie. He was another strong and constant presence in my life, and we still have a great relationship today. I have chosen great friends for myself because of my father's example and that of his friends.

At twenty-two, I made the decision to walk in my faith, and that's when my relationship with my dad grew even closer. We continue to have a fun, loving relationship today. What I wished for as a child has come true. He has been a prophetic voice in my life. He was there when I went to college to further my education, and he was there through my graduate studies. He fully supported my decision to serve God, first as a minister and then onto become a pastor. When I retired as a pastor to work on my global ministry initiatives, he was my biggest supporter and contributed generously to the causes that God lead me to pursue! I am the man I am today and have the relationship I have with God today because of the exceptional example I had in Robert Earl, Sr. throughout my life. I was blessed with five beautiful children - two of them sons - and now, we have four generations of Earls. My dad's example continues to influence us all.

Dr. Anthony Earl

BISHOP CHARLES ELLIS

Bishop Charles H. Ellis III is the Senior Pastor of Greater Grace Temple, referred to as the City of David in Detroit, Michigan. He served 8 years as the Presiding Prelate of the Pentecostal Assemblies of the World, Incorporated (the world's oldest Apostolic Reformation in modern history). Bishop Ellis currently serves on many Detroit area corporate boards and is also a respected influential leader throughout the country.

MY GREAT EXAMPLE

My dad and I could share laughs, shoot billiards, play ping pong, baseball, Scrabble, and many other enjoyable games and activities together. I always knew he was the parent, and I was the child. That never diminished, even when I became a man leading my own family. My dad demanded respect as the head of the house, and I never even thought about challenging him. He was a tremendous provider and encouraged me to accomplish great things in life.

His presence in our home was like a huge shadow of protection covering every square foot of our home. Just knowing that he was in his bedroom or in the family room watching television gave me that comfort of safety and security. Whenever he traveled to minister out of town, I felt somewhat uncovered and anxious until he returned. The fact that my father was in my life is an understatement. My dad wanted to know everything about my life. He wanted to know who I was befriending, and about my girlfriend relationships. He was very much on top of my school grades and conduct, just to name a few things. In short, he wanted to know where I was, where I was going, and who I was with.

My father was a great example of a true man and leader. I say this in respect to his Godly principles, which shaped his integrity with regard to his various roles as husband, father, pastor, friend to many, and surrogate to numerous children whose fathers were absent in their lives. I would say that probably his greatest example to me was demonstrated in the love that he had for everyone.

I would honestly say that I feel somewhat fulfilled in my role as a man as a result of the measure of success that I have achieved. My father taught me strongly that each person must create their own legacy and not merely attempt to live off of other's.

I believe without a doubt that I have raised my children true to the principles that my father set in our home. His principles served as the benchmark and course, and I have made the necessary adjustments to adapt to this age and time.

I have many fond memories of my dad, but some of my fondest

memories are during my childhood. We attended events such as the circus, wrestling, baseball games, football games, church picnics, and ice capades. The holidays were always very special. We attended the Detroit Lions football games on Thanksgiving Day after the early morning Thanksgiving Day services, and exchanged presents during Christmas. Having extended family and church friends over the house to enjoy food, games, and fun was always something to look forward to.

He taught me many life lessons that have guided me to this day. I know today how important it was to learn the difference between right and wrong. His talks and conversations while riding in the car on honesty, integrity, and good moral character remain with me to this day.

I believe a big part of who my father was came from his father. Bishop David Lee Ellis, Sr. was a second-generation Pentecostal pastor, born and raised in Chicago, Illinois in the aftermath of the Great Depression. His family was a functional two-parent home and his mom tended to the family needs within the home. My dad was 18 years old when his father died of a heart attack at 53 years of age.

He often spoke of his father as a role model and mentor from whom he learned many invaluable lessons. Some instructions and corrections he caught through conversations and many others he received through "chastening." This relationship was cemented in respect and appreciation of their roles. The home atmosphere was saturated with Godly principles and an utmost respect for God and church.

My grandfather was a full-time pastor, but also worked a daily job selling fruit from his pickup truck. This second job was necessary for him to adequately provide for his family that included ten children. Due to the toll of these obligations, he often spent much of each day outside of the home. Therefore, my father had as much time with his dad during church services than at home.

I never heard my dad speak with any disrespect concerning his father. He always spoke in terms of desiring to remain in Chicago to assist his dad throughout his lifetime. I felt like my dad had a close relationship with his father, and that helped shape our relationship.

I am so thankful for the time and many lessons I learned from my father. I realize there are so many men out there who were not as blessed as I was to have their fathers at home and to have the great relationship I had with my dad. For this, I am truly grateful.

NEIL BORDEN

Neil Borden, retired Metropolitan Atlanta Rapid Transit Authority, Operations Supervisor, working for 27 years in the field. Upon retirement, he resumed a previous part time business, "Neil's fix it for sure" a general repair/restoration service, specializing in home upgrades. He is married to Nora Shariff-Borden "my childhood sweetheart" and they have 6 children, 13 grandchildren, and 1 great grandchild.

THE MAN I ADMIRED

My mother and father were married on April 10, 1945 in Boston, Massachusetts. They went on to have 13 children together. Unfortunately, my brother Robert died from SIDS (Sudden infant Death Syndrome). In the early years of my life, I remember having a great relationship with my father. He was home unless he was working. He was playful, and he enjoyed painting, drawing, and listening to classical music. I remember wanting to be like him, so much so that I even attempted to walk like him one day. He said, "No, son, don't walk like that."

My father seemed to always be around when he wasn't at work, and it was great! You see, my mother was the disciplinarian, and he was the talker and the explainer. I can remember one day my dad caught me calling someone a faggot when I was with my friends. He took me home and asked if I even knew what a faggot was. I said no, and he went on to explain to me that a faggot was just a piece of wood. Now, knowing what it meant, I never used the word again. Well, I later found out that the word actually didn't mean a piece of wood; it was just a tactic he used to get me to stop saying it. He was smart like that. There were times that he would just show up out of nowhere when I happened to be misbehaving, like when my friends and I were hopping on the back of the street cars. I was having the time of my life until I heard someone yell out, "Here comes Mr. Borden!" I jumped off that bus so fast and ended up rolling into the street. The bus was going too fast for me to catch my balance, and I'm sure you can guess who was standing over me when I finally came to a stop. Yes, my father! He picked me up and carried me to the sidewalk. He asked if I was hurt and then proceeded to explain just how dangerous that was.

My dad was an only child. His father died when he was very young, so he never got the chance to know him. My grandmother never remarried, but always remained very close to my dad and our family until her death on January 20, 1997. She was 98 years old. My father drank. When he did, there was chaos. I saw it as excitement and didn't realize that his drinking was a problem until years later, when it got worse. We lived on the third floor of our apartment building. One evening, I heard my mother screaming outside in the hallway. I walked out to see what was going on. When I looked over the railing, I saw my father fighting with three or four Boston police officers. It was hard to watch! He was drunk and trying to fight all of them by himself until they finally took him down. My parents moved the family from Back Bay, a mixed community, to Roxbury, which is considered the hood. Nevertheless, we were excited because my parents purchased a home with a lot more space for us, along with a yard. We were excited to have new friends and neighbors. During the next three or four years and through my pre-teens, my father drifted further and further away, both physically and emotionally. He drank alcohol more and more, and when he drank, he stayed away from home for days at a time. When he did come home, he was so intoxicated that he fell asleep. When he woke up, he just looked for more alcohol. My father was an alcoholic.

One day he left home. I'm not sure if he left on his own or if he was forced to leave by my mother. I wanted to talk to him, so she told me that he was at work, and that's where I could find him. My younger brother Rick and I went to find my dad. He worked not too far from our home. When we talked to him, he explained to us that before he could come back home, he had to get better, and that he wasn't exactly sure when that would be. He gave us his new address and said that whenever we needed him, we could come to his job or to his new apartment. I really wanted to know how long it would be until he got better and came back home, but he couldn't tell me because he didn't know how long getting better would take. All he could say was, "I will be back."

I missed my father. I missed him being there talking to me. I missed him catching me when I was doing something I shouldn't be doing. It seemed that he was gone forever, but in reality, it was just a few years. My friends felt the void of my dad's absence. I made new friends from the projects called Orchard Park, and we got better acquainted. We roamed the streets of Boston looking for things to get into - usually trouble - and then, one day someone shouted, "There goes Mr. Borden!" I saw my father staggering down the street drunk. It was a common occurrence to see him intoxicated on the street or coming out of a bar, at times with another woman. I sometimes helped him get into a cab, but there were also times when he told me to leave him alone. I was embarrassed to see him drunk in public.

Even though my father was gone from the house, I had friends with no fathers at all. That made me appreciate my dad, even though he was going through some life changes. I just felt good about at least having a dad. Nevertheless, there were times I was on my own, at least until my father recovered from his alcoholism. I had my friends, but we were on a scary road, headed for a life of danger, anger, drugs, alcohol, and becoming high school dropouts. Together, we had many late nights, fights, and plenty of guns and girls. By the looks of things, instead of preparing to graduate from high school and go to college, we were preparing ourselves to go to jail or - worse - heading to the funeral home. Of course, none of this happened overnight. In the time that my father was out of the house, I became knee-deep in a life that I felt instant gratification from. Seeing my father in the street wasn't going to change that.

My father did eventually return home to his wife and nine children. By then, my two older siblings had moved out, and my youngest sibling would be born the following year. After returning home to his family, my dad was doing great! He was thriving! He even went back to school and received his bachelor's and master's degrees, and he was dedicated to helping his community. He began working for the Roxbury District Court as a Drug and Alcohol Advocate. He also joined the Kiwanis Club of Roxbury, as well as served with the Salvation Army of Roxbury, and, he sat on the board of The Roxbury Multi-Service Center as well. He was instrumental in developing a Detox Program in the community, serving as the Director of The Roxbury Detox Center, and it doesn't stop there! My father also went on to work for the Suffolk County Sheriff's Department as a Deputy Sheriff in the Boston Superior Court House. My dad had, in fact, made a full recovery from the disease known as alcoholism, and he never touched a single drop of that poison for the rest of his life.

On December 18, 2010, his life here with us ended. I am so glad he was able to help and see me recover from my reckless life. For that, I am forever thankful to him. He was there for me when I needed him. I didn't recognize it at the time, but our lives were pretty much the same. Although my father did not know his dad, he learned how to be a great father! I wish that I could've provided my children with what he provided to me. I don't think I was able to heal and work through the pain I felt.

At one point, I remember feeling really hurt and angry at my dad. Instead of telling him how I felt, I kept those feelings and hurt inside of me, and I carried that pain with me for many years. I am so glad that God blessed me with my beautiful wife Nora. She has supported me through my recovery and has been an instrumental part of my healing! We've known one another since the sixth grade. She was the flower of my youth, and the apple of my eye. We dated twice during our teenage years, and I always knew God had plans for us. Those plans were confirmed when he brought us back together as adults, and it has been my greatest honor, I am proud to say I have had a loving relationship with her, and it has been over 40 beautiful years of love. God would have it that she would be my wife for the rest of my life.

RODNEY HOWELL

Rodney Howell, is a Detroit, Michigan native.   An Entrepreneur, who possess many talents, such as   interior design, fashion stylist, philanthropist, and the owner of Hairshion and Silver Fox Salons.

A DICTATORSHIP

My relationship with my father was more of a dictatorship. Being raised in the 60s was totally different. You did what you were told, and you didn't stray from that, or there would be major consequences. I respected my dad, but I was also afraid of him. He was strict; however, there was always a sense of security with him being in the home. I saw him as a strong, powerful man.

There was nothing my dad couldn't do in my eyes. He worked several jobs to provide for our big family, so even though he was living in the home, he was gone a lot. He still made himself available for the important things, like going to school meetings with our teachers, because he was serious about our education! He was the one who helped me with my homework. He was very good at math and history. I thought he was the smartest man in the world. He just didn't have much patience, which made me afraid to get homework problems wrong. He made sure that I studied hard and got it right.

My father was more of a provider and a disciplinarian. He didn't show his love in an affectionate way, and I am sure that was because he did not receive the love and affection that he needed from his father. The best way he knew how to show his love was by making sure we had what we needed. He showed it by teaching my brothers and me how to be men, how to work with our hands, and what a man should do to provide for himself and his family. He instilled values and responsibility in us.

Although I never had any children of my own, I believe that because of all that my father instilled in me, I know that I would have made a great father. I had the privilege of raising my 7 year old nephew for several years, and that was very rewarding for me. I was strict and stern with him, just like my dad was with me, but I do believe that showing your children love makes a difference. The thing that I remember most about my dad is that he was a man of integrity. He was a no-nonsense man who was very serious about providing for his family and being an example for my brothers and me. He wanted to make sure we were strong men who were able to provide for ourselves. Back then, I didn't understand him or the way he was. Today, I am so appreciative that he was there to raise us. He looked up to his dad and respected him, and he taught us to do the same for him! Thanks, Dad!

GERARD R. LEWIS

A husband, a father and an entrepreneur, Gerard R. Lewis migrated to America from the beautiful Island of Trinidad, as a young teen. He went on to pursue a career in computer operations and accounting. He met the love of his life in High School, and they have been married for 32 years, and are the proud parents of two children.

IN MY FATHERS ABSENCE

I grew up with my father, but it was my mother who ruled the household. The majority of my friends came from single-family households, and I was one of the few who had both parents at home. Even though my father lived with us, he worked a lot and wasn't really present. My oldest brother took the role of the man of the house in my father's absence. He even attended my sporting events because my father couldn't. In the West Indian culture, the oldest takes care of the younger siblings. Therefore, my three older brothers and I raised each other and our younger sisters. There was no need for any other father figures. From the time I started working at the age of 16, I was committed to helping my mother pay the bills. When my two older brothers went into the armed services, my third oldest brother and I stepped up to provide for our two younger sisters. I learned from a young age to make sure that my family was always taken care of. I know that experience helped to shape how I would eventually care for and love my own family. I made sure that I was always present in my children's lives. I didn't miss a school event, sports event, or anything else my children were a part of. I was there. I made a conscious decision to not just be a provider, but to also understand the importance of having a great relationship with my children. I remember how I felt when my parents divorced and my father chose to not speak to us for years. That was heart breaking to me, and it is because of that experience that I made sure to always be there for my family, to make sure they are well taken care of, and to make sure they know I love them.

KENNETH DALE MONDAY

First African American to win a USA Gold medal in Wrestling. Hall of Famer, born and raised in Tulsa, OK. Head Coach, Tar Heel Wrestling Club - UNC Chapel Hill, NC. Married 26 yrs., Sabrina Goodwin Monday. Three college educated young adult children: Sydnee, Howard University; Kennedy, UNC Chapel Hill; and Quincy, Princeton University.

A STRONG PRESENCE

My earliest memories of my father were around the age of four or five. My father, Fred Monday, was a strong presence in our home. I'm the youngest of three boys, so I was able to watch my older brothers and navigate what I could and could not do in order to stay on my dad's good side. My father was moderately strict, but good natured. We had fun times, laughing and joking with each other. He always gave me the freedom to grow and make friends and develop relationships. I got involved with sports early in life. 90% of my life revolved around school and sports. My dad was always supportive. He stressed that if I start a sport, I must be committed and finish whatever I start. I had a great support system at home. My dad made sure I didn't miss a practice or a game! It taught me early on how to be disciplined and accountable. He also taught me from an early age how to stand up for myself. At the age of five, I started wrestling at the YMCA after school program in Tulsa, Oklahoma. Most of the kids were older and bigger than me, but I was never afraid to speak up for myself. I fell in love with the sport of wrestling, so much so that my parents helped to create a wrestling team of neighborhood kids called The Skull Crushers. We travelled around the state and made a name for ourselves. My parents were instrumental in my success in life because of their belief, support, and all they instilled in me. I believe that gave me a huge advantage in life. One of the most important lessons my father instilled in me was how to be respectful in every way and to all people, especially to adults. I always referred to an adult as Mr. or Mrs., and never on a first name basis; it just wasn't tolerated. He taught me to be respectful to everyone, including my coaches, teammates, and the sport itself. Most importantly, we were taught to RESPECT OURSELVES. That meant being confident in who I was, never backing down from a challenge, and knowing my own capabilities. My dad taught me to work hard, prepare myself, and be humble, in victory or defeat. The foundation my father set provided me with the basic principles that I live my life by today. I have a strong faith in God and dedication to my family and friends. I believe in myself, I set goals, I dream big, and I learned to go after those dreams with everything that I have in me. That is the foundation that my wife and I have raised our children on.

I am the man that I am today because of my dad's example. He taught me that in order to create a life well lived, one must put in the work to create that desired life. No man is perfect, including my father. Yes, he made mistakes, but it was because of those mistakes that I was able to learn from and become a better man through his experiences. As a child, I never saw him late for work or miss a day. His work ethic was unmatched. He would always say, "Take care of business first," whether that was school, work, practice, or chores around the house.

I will always remember this one particular conversation my dad and I had. I was ten and had just lost a match that I believed I should have won. The referee made some bad calls against me, and I came off the mat upset and emotional. He sat me down and explained to me that you can take control of the situation by working harder, being more focused, and not allowing bad calls by the referee to determine the outcome of the match. That was the conversation that defined my wrestling career and is the reason that I was able to win an Olympic Gold Medal in Seoul, Korea in 1988, becoming the first African American to win an Olympic Gold Medal. That same YMCA that I first started wrestling at, The Hutcherson YMCA, now resides on Kenny Monday Place, a street named in my honor.

I am happy to say that today, my dad is 83 years old and is still vibrant! I'm proud to carry on the MONDAY Man legacy, and I'm blessed that I have two sons who will continue to hold that name and make a difference in the world.

PASTOR JOHN NEWMAN

John Allen Newman for 37 years has served as the Senior Pastor of The Sanctuary at Mt. Calvary Church in Jacksonville, Florida. He shares together joyfully in marriage and ministry with his wife the Rev. Omarosa Manigault Newman. Pastor Newman has a Bachelor's Degree in Religion from Eastern University, a Masters in Theological Studies from Palmer Theological Seminary, an Honorary Doctorate Divinity from Virginia Seminary and is a Doctor of Ministry candidate at Ashland Theological Seminary, Ashland, Ohio.

A TREMENDOUS RELATIONSHIP

I was blessed to have a tremendous relationship with my father. Both of my parents were older when they had me. My father was 53, and my mother was 41. This afforded me the blessing of being raised with a value system that reflected their wisdom and years of experience. Those values were spiritual, economic, and social.

My father was chairman of the deacons of my home church, and for a significant period of time, our congregation was without pastoral leadership. My father had the responsibility of helping to keep the church together during that difficult time. I saw him do this with integrity and authenticity. He saw himself as a steward of the Lord's church, and I observed this to be true. My father led us in prayer at home. He and my mother set the spiritual atmosphere and tone in our home. We prayed, and we worshipped together. Jesus was deeply loved in our family, and the model of Christ in our home helped influence me to follow Christ later in my own life.

I also saw how hard my father worked to provide for us. He worked every day at a lumber supply company. One of my fondest memories was when I accompanied my father to work. We often returned at night to help my mother clean the office building, something we did for extra income. My father was no stranger to hard work. He had to drop out of school to raise his younger siblings when his parents passed away. His brothers and sisters even referred to him affectionately as Pop. Another precious memory I have with my father was walking through the shopping centers in our hometown during the Christmas season. I watched him ask all the store owners if he could place our "Keep Christ in Christmas" signs in their windows.

One night, the doorbell rang, and I climbed out of bed to peek down the steps to look at the front door. I saw a man talking to my father, but I couldn't hear what they were saying. The next day, I asked my mother about the man who rang our doorbell. She told me that it was a young man who had been released from jail into my father's custody. She also told me that he was not the only one. My father gave these men an opportunity to change their lives and help him at the same time. That's the kind of man my father was, and that's the kind of guidance I grew up under. He was not only a man of faith, but one who exemplified his faith in a Christ-like way.

Faith was at the center of our relationship. My father and I got up early every Sunday morning to attend the men's fellowship breakfast at our church. We also gathered at other churches when they were celebrating "Men's Day." Then, we returned in time for Sunday service at our home church. It was in that same sanctuary, with that same congregation, that I preached my first sermon at just 17 years old when I was called into ministry. My father was never prouder of me.

Sadly, two years later, my father's life ended from a heart attack early one Monday morning. My father was an amazing example of Christian manhood. Although he was a man short in stature physically, he was a giant in so many ways. No matter the accomplishments I've achieved, I will never be half the man that he was, but he left a legacy, and I continue to strive to be the kind of man he would be proud of.

ASIM OSAZE

Husband, father, son, cousin and friend. Videographer, photographer, producer, entrepreneur. Content creator, communication specialist at the University of Illinois Urbana-Champaign.

EXPRESSING LOVE

My father is a Muslim and a very no-nonsense kind of person. I don't recall him physically or verbally expressing his love, but it was clear in his actions. He was always there. I could always and still can depend on him for anything. He was very adamant that I did well in school, as he was knowledgeable about many things. African American history is his favorite subject. His friends were Black Panthers, and he made sure to impart that knowledge on to me and my friends. He always told me to be careful about the people I hung around, and he made it a point to always meet my friends. He was always direct when talking to me. He would tell me where some of my friends would end up.

I remember him telling my friends, who also looked up to him, "Asim is my son, and it is my job to protect him and make sure he does the right thing. You're his friends. I can't control what you do, but I can and will control what he does".

My friends always respected my dad, and I believe they feared him, too. I think that's why they didn't let me get into any of their crazy stuff. My father was the type of person who commanded respect without even speaking. I would have felt unprotected and unsafe if I didn't have my father in the home growing up in Chicago. I also wouldn't have had anyone to keep me on the straight and narrow path.

I didn't realize how important it was to have my father home until I got older. I was around 10 or 12 years old when my bike was stolen. It was summer, and my dad was at work. I was outside at my grandparent's house riding my bike with a childhood friend when we were approached by some older kids, who took our bikes. After buying new bikes with my older cousin, my dad and my grandfather, we saw the guys who stole our bikes. Now my dad was pretty big, and he was all muscle. My cousin was home from the Army. They grabbed those guys, and we went to the police station, but nothing was done about it. That's when I saw firsthand that the system was useless for people like us, but it's also when I saw firsthand how far my family would go to protect me! I guess that explains why I'm overprotective of my own family today.

I didn't always make the best decisions, but having a father to answer to made the difference between me being here now or being dead or in

jail. My dad has always worn suits and his Kufi, even to this day. I think he may own one or two pairs of jeans and sneakers. He kept to himself and never ran with a crew. Now, I understand why. Many of his friends that were Panthers were framed and sent to prison while he was in the military, but he never treated them any differently. He has friends who fell victim to substance abuse, but he never turned his back on them.
If I had not had the living example of my father to emulate, I believe growing up in Chicago would have been disastrous for me. I truly don't believe I'd be where I am today without him.

I could not have had a better example. My father led us like a King! He is royalty, as was my grandfather. I want to be like these two men. There are so many ways he led that I can't mention them all. My father and grandfather never took shortcuts. They weren't risk takers. I grew up hearing "Hope for the best, but prepare for the worst." It's so much a part of me that my kids hear it and lovingly sigh and roll their eyes, just like I did.

The best way to explain how he was a great example is that he did not just tell me – he showed me. He is a living example, simple and plain. He is always there to answer any question, to help with homework, protect, defend. He was always there - no matter what. Now he's that for my son and daughter. It's amazing to me to watch them with each other. They can't go a day without talking to him. Any shortcomings I had as a man are because of me. My father gave me everything I needed to go out into the world. It was up to me to implement what I learned from him and apply it. Did I always do so? No. Is that my father's fault? Not by any means. My father is proud of me, maybe more so than I am of myself. He was the first child to graduate college, and I was the second. I added an MBA years later, and I am currently considering a second master's degree!

He did the best he could with what he knew. In many ways, I'm like my father. We have similar mannerisms: seriousness, very reserved, analytical, and methodical. My father's foundation is based on the traditions and experiences of his parents and generational beliefs. The foundation my children have learned is a continuation of the morals and principles instilled in me.

My father was always present both physically and mentally. He has always been there for family if they need him. He never let anything or any commitment come between us. I could count on my father for anything, He loved me no matter how badly I messed up. My dad wasn't much for expressing his feelings, but I knew I could feel it. He does say now that he wished he'd verbally expressed and shown more affection. He just didn't know how, because he didn't experience it much. I can't think of any real complaints to speak to; he was always there when I needed him without question. He supported me no matter what. He always had my back and held me down. He also knew when to let go and allow me to learn life lessons on my own, even though it was hard for him.

My father was very close to his father as well. My grandfather and my father are the two most outstanding men I know. Anything I have learned about life - the good and the bad - I learned from them. I have so many memories of them and us together. My dad stopped by his parents' house every day without fail. My grandfather taught my dad how to fish, hunt, drive, and everything in between. He taught me those same lessons, along with reinforcing what my father taught me. He was incredible. The one difference between the two was that grandpa wasn't as serious as dad. Dad got that from my grandma. I was 30 when my grandfather passed away. That was the first time I saw my dad cry. I felt helpless, because I didn't know what to say or do. I never saw my dad vulnerable like that, and I just didn't know how to respond. I ended up going outside and crying myself, along with my family. I guess we all figured he'd be here forever.

One of my best memories with my grandfather was while I was in college. I had a history assignment to interview someone who lived through the Great Depression. Naturally, I chose my grandfather. It was the best thing I could have done! The interview had to be audio recorded. Even though my grandfather isn't here with us anymore, I still have him on tape telling his life story for three to four hours for my class interview. That was truly one of my greatest memories of my grandfather.

VOP OSILI

Vop Osili is an architect who has for many years led urban design and architecture projects throughout the U.S., Africa and the Middle East. He currently serves as President of the Indianapolis City-County Council where, first elected to the Council in 2011, he has focused on addressing issues of race and equity, reentry, affordable housing, homelessness, police/community engagement, and inclusive urban development. Osili graduated from Carnegie-Mellon University with a bachelor's degree in architecture and from Columbia University with a master's degree in architecture and urban design. He and his wife Una are the proud parents of two amazing children, Arinze and Tasia.

MY BELOVED FATHER

I loved, respected, and honored my father very much. Our relationship in my childhood was a more traditional one of a son to a beloved father. It wasn't intimate, but respectful and admiring. As I grew into adulthood and got to know him as a person, not just as a father, my relationship with him and my admiration for him blossomed. I always felt safe and protected having my father in the home.

I was four years old when my mother brought my two sisters and me to America to escape the civil war in Nigeria. My father made the decision to stay and contribute to the war, a decision no one knew at the time would be the start of a five-year separation. I felt my father's absence, even at just four years old. The plan was to stay with my mother's family in America until the war was over. When I was nine, the civil war was over, and we returned to Nigeria. At first, it was difficult to relate to what seemed to be a new culture and environment, but my father made sure we knew we would be together again as a family.

My father was always an amazing example in my life. In my youth, I witnessed his character and dignity by the respect he showed others and the honor and reverence shown by others to him. I admired him and the self-discipline he exhibited. What I remember most about my childhood is the structure and stability of our home. My parents held each other in high regard and showed a level of warmth and respect and honor to one another that I have seldom witnessed over the course of my life. Our home was beautiful, peaceful, and a place I always felt safe.

As I grew into adulthood and began to know him more intimately, I understood him as more than a good and loving father, but as someone with heartfelt compassion for the welfare of others. He always used his abilities to affect a positive outcome in others' lives. His example is likely at the root of what led me into the field of politics. I feel that I had the very best possible role model as a father.

My father's character and actions exhibited amazing discipline, compassion, and thoughtfulness. He was a man of matured thinking, and I try to draw upon his example every day of my life. It has set a strong foundation for how I raised my own children. I see the raising of my children as one of love and one of setting expectations of behavior and purpose. And, while always trying to ensure that my children know that I love them and will always have a sympathetic and compassionate ear for their issues and concerns, I see that, as a father, it is more important to be a parent than a pal.

My father was a rather quiet man who held a very powerful position in government. His very presence was calm, strong, and reassuring. Our house was a quiet gathering place, a safe haven for my family and friends. My father was a very compassionate man who listened intensely to concerns and issues and thoughtfully offered his feedback. As a child, I saw my father through others' eyes and admired him as they did. I saw the ways he provided support and the quiet dignity he showed to everyone. As I grew older and asked more questions, he willingly shared his way of thinking, his reasoning, and his motivations. Then, I respected and admired him even more.

My more personal memories of my father and me together were not over sports or other activities. Instead, these memories are of more quiet affairs like talking at a table or him going over papers from the office while I did my homework. I asked him questions, and he listened and answered them. He was always patient. Because he was brilliant in math, I believed it rubbed off on me and became my favorite subject. It was at these times I came to learn more about the man he was, and these are the times I remember most.

CHARLES TUCKER

Charles Tucker is a second-generation Cape Verdean American, raised in Roxbury, MA. He retired in 2011 after working 33 years in the airline industry and now reside on Cape Cod. In 2017, he returned to work as a clinician helping people struggling with opiate addiction.

A MAN OF FEW WORDS

Although my father was a man of few words, I had a great relationship with him. He wasn't particularly strict and left most of the discipline to my mother, but he was no pushover. I found that out at 16 when I thought to raise my hand to him. Even though I was always a good fighter in the streets, my father showed me I wasn't as good as I thought I was, and he beat me like a rug. That's when I realized he had fight training, and that's why he left discipline to my mom.

He was present for all my activities growing up, particularly baseball. My dad was a great baseball player, and he taught me the game from the young age of three. He played for the Boston Wolverines, which was the best semiprofessional black baseball team in New England. I became the most accomplished pitcher to come out of a black Boston community during the mid-sixties. He was intensely proud of my games, and he attended almost all of them.

He always set the example that family came first. He worked 5 1/2 days every week as a meat cutter in the meat district at Faneuil Hall. I found out how physically demanding his job was when he got me a job with him the summer before I attended Howard University. I only lasted one week! I followed the example he set of working to take care of your family. He sacrificed everything for his children and led by example.
What I remember most is his strong work ethic and his attention to good grooming. He was a good dresser and had nice jewelry and fine suits, though he rarely dressed up. He also didn't believe in loaning or borrowing money. He believed that was the quickest way to ruin a friendship. When I saw him give someone money, he said he didn't expect it back.

I learned nothing of my father's upbringing from him. All the information I got was from his sister. His father was Sicilian and never lived with my grandmother. He had two brothers and a sister. For a time, he lived outside of Pittsburgh, Pennsylvania. His mother was originally from Virginia. His mother died when he was nine, and he bounced around with relatives and orphanages. He even spent time at a home for Native American children. He had an extremely hard upbringing because of his complexion. The only thing I knew he did besides play baseball was work. I found out at his funeral that he was a really good saxophone player who regularly sat in with famous bands at Connally's and the Hi Hat club. I also found out that he was a champion roller skater and accomplished horseback rider. He taught people how to ride on the beaches of Atlantic City when he lived there before moving to Boston. He never spoke of those things.

Although my parents would occasionally argue over things, I never saw him hit or disrespect my mother in any way. That lesson was not a lost one. We loved him dearly. One short story I want to share happened when I was twelve and in the sixth grade. I became a Boy Scout, and one day I was told that I needed to wear the uniform to school the next day. After working his 6:30am shift at the market, my dad still found the time to take me to Jordan Marsh, a clothing store in downtown Boston, in a snow storm! The storm shut down buses, so we had to walk in the snow all the way home. We didn't get home until 10:00pm, all so my mother could sew the patches on the uniform that I had to wear to school the next morning. He was special. I owe my great relationship with my three daughters and son, along with six grandchildren, to the example the that he set for me.

CHUCK WILLIAMSON, PHD

Dr. Chuck Williamson is an educator and retired law enforcement officer, currently serving as Dean of the School of Public Service and Administration at Anderson University in Anderson, South Carolina. Dr. Williamson is a researcher and consultant in the areas of leader development, organization change, and public policy. Dr. Williamson has served his Lord and Savior Jesus Christ as a member of Evangel Fellowship COGIC for 30 years, where he serves as ordained Elder. He is married to Beth for 30 years and they have three sons; Cory (27), Chase (23), and Camden (22).

WINNING IN SPITE OF ADVERSITY

I had a very good relationship with my father. He was just 18 years old when I was born. He was very athletic and played baseball at North Carolina A&T University. I can remember traveling with my dad to softball tournaments as early as when I was five or six years old. We spent a lot of time together on these trips. I enjoyed traveling with him, eating out, and staying in hotels. It was fun to me. If he was playing in town, I spent the weekends with him at the ball field. I got to watch my father play, and I learned some things about work ethic, hustle, team play, and working to win in spite of adversity.

I remember when we went to a softball tournament in North Carolina in the early 1970's. I was listening to a conversation my father was having with the tournament director and the coach of my dad's team. The director told his coach that my dad couldn't play because "niggers" weren't allowed to play in Level Cross, NC, and my father was the only black player on the team. At the time, I did not understand the situation, but I did have an understanding of the derogatory nature of the term "nigger." The coach told the tournament director that if my father couldn't play, the team wouldn't play. Softball was a very popular sport in North Carolina at the time, and my father's team, Higgins Cyclery, was a nationally ranked team. They drew a crowd wherever they played. Ultimately, the tournament director agreed to let my father play.

I remember how tense the entire weekend was (at least for me). My father normally allowed me to roam the ball parks and play with other kids; however, this weekend, he made me stay in the dugout with the team. I wondered if someone was going to try to hurt us. My father played the entire weekend, and it didn't seem to affect him. I asked my father why they didn't like us. He told me that it didn't matter whether anybody liked us, and we should not be intimidated by anyone just because we are black. That was one of the earliest lessons I can remember learning from my father, and it still follows me today.

My father was an educator. He taught physical education to middle and high school students. He also coached a number of sports, including football, wrestling, and baseball for middle and high school. He was my football and baseball coach in middle and high school. I love the fact that my father was always present. We spent a lot of time together, and he supported me in everything I did.

I guess the best word that I could use in retrospect to describe how his presence made me feel would be "secure." I don't recall ever having to worry about where my next meal was coming from or whether we had the things I needed, because my father always provided for his family. I am so thankful that he created a safe home environment for me. My father is a great example of what a good father and husband should be.

He wasn't perfect, but he was hard working. He owned his own taxi, he was a summer camp coach, and he worked part-time as a basketball official. He also supported other people outside of his family, like his students and kids that played on his teams. The schools I attended were inner city and minority. We always had other kids with us going to practices and games, and he almost always took kids out to dinner and provided meals after practices and games. His former players still ask me how he's doing and tell me stories about him keeping them on the straight and narrow. He always had a good relationship with them.

My father definitely set a strong foundation for how I raised my boys. I try to model his presence. I've tried to be there and support my young men as they have grown and matriculated into adult life.

My dad didn't talk about his father much. My grandfather was killed at the age of 53, when I was 9 years old. It was extremely painful for him, but he never let that pain get in the way of raising me. I thank him for that.

Winning in spite of adversity is the key to success! One is never paralyzed by life obstacles. The key is to focus on the things you can control vs the things you can't. One thing about adversity is it can and will build character in a fighter.

"There is no better than adversity. Every defeat, every heartbreak, every loss, contains its own seed, its own lesson on how to improve your performance the next time."
— MALCOLM X

"The gem cannot be polished without friction, nor woman perfected without trials."
— CHINESE PROVERB

I loved how my dad handled the adversity of racism. He was determined not to let the actions of others destroy his winning! There was a key lesson for me that day and that was "you are in control of how you respond to negative situations."

ROLE MODEL

My experience is people usually live what they learn.

Meaning some men don't have good fathers as a role model. Sad but true.

For the ones who grew up with great fathers, yet turn out to be careless fathers,there is no excuse for them.

Then there are those wonderful men who were raised by a bad father. They somehow have learned from that bad experience. They become great fathers **despite** the lack of a good father role model.

A Dad Is The Best Role Model

A Dad Isn't Afraid To Cry

A Dad Is Always There To Protect His Children

A Dad Will Always Keep His Child's Imagination Wild

A Dad Isn't Asked To Spend Time With His Children

A Dad Loves Family Time

A Dad Won't Put Friends Before Family

Dads Don't Have To Be Asked To Take Care Of Their Children

A Dad Will Do Anything For His Children

A Dad Will Never Stop Protecting His Child

- Nora Shariff Borden

TYRONE LAWSON

Tyrone Lawson is originally from Queens, NY. He is a graduate from North Carolina A&T. Tyrone is a committed husband to his college sweetheart and wife Aminah. They have two amazing sons Tahir and Ja'el, They reside in Greensboro, NC.

GROWING UP WITHOUT A FATHER

My feelings of growing up without my father was that of normality at first. The majority of my friends and family also did not have a father in the home, with the exception of a few foreign families I knew who said it was their culture for their father to be in the home. This subsequently defined my fatherless upbringing and the countless others as a culture I was in. I never felt weird or bad about seeing my friends who had fathers in the home, because I was convinced that it was a cultural thing, and that's just the way it was supposed to be.

When I was a teenager, it became clear why my father was not in the home. He had a dysfunctional relationship with my mother. It wasn't an abusive relationship, but it was a relationship that I realized was just not normal. It became clear to me that they had no covenant of marriage, which created confusion in me. I began to believe that I didn't need to be married to someone, and that we could just operate in a dysfunctional relationship, as I watched my parents do for years. I began to form the idea that I never needed or wanted to be married, and I didn't want to have children in order to spare them the life of dysfunction that I lived. Although they didn't live in harmony, my mother never created a hateful image or spoke a regretful word about my father. We remained very close to his side of the family and my sisters, his two daughters from a previous marriage.

We had a very strong family community. Although it was made up of mostly women, they ensured that I was aware of who I was as a man and how men should conduct themselves, according to them as women. They wanted to assure that my self-esteem and worth was clear to me from the perspective of women who knew how they wanted to be treated by men. They did a great a job of distracting me from negative feelings that might have caused me to devalue myself for not being able to do father-son activities with my dad. I do remember my father teaching me how to ride a bike without training wheels, and that memory sticks with me to this day. I was able to experience with my dad easily one of the defining moments of transitioning from a child into a young man. Riding a bike without training wheels like all the big boys is a pivotal moment. When your father is the one to teach you, it is the ultimate validation. You feel like a man, or a least a big boy. I hold this memory and reflect on it in times when I have those negative or devalued thoughts about other missed opportunities for my father to validate me as a man. I remind myself that at least he was there for that one.

I never related my father's absence in my life to pain. Therefore, I never felt the need to use any kind of substance to deal with such an emotion. I may have felt some anger, then some remorse, and finally empathy for my dad, but nothing beyond that. As an only child, I dove inward, retreating to my thoughts and allowing my imagination and love for comics, music, and art to create a space of comfort and peace.

I approached my relationship with my sons with the mindset that I was not going to be like my father. I constantly evaluated my actions based on what my father did or didn't do, determined to do the opposite. At the end of the day, I am who I am because my father is who he is. We are not the same, so I had to walk in my own shoes as a father. Initially, I allowed my upbringing to impact the way I started to raise my children. I told myself that I'm not going to do this or that because my father did it. Soon, I realized that I was not operating in my own abilities as a father. I was casting a mental shadow of negative thoughts about my father, and, truth be told, my father was a good man. He was smart. Everyone liked him and had nothing but good things to say about him. The moments we shared together at various stages in my life really did hold value. I also had a great support system, and they raised me to become the man I am today. I was adequate and well-equipped to complete being a good father, and I didn't have to think poorly of my dad to do it.

My mother never remarried or even had intimate relationships with any other men. She made sure that any of her male friends were a positive example. My parents shared the same circle of friends. The men in that circle looked after me and were all men that I could admire. As far as a father figure, I honestly didn't want one or feel that I needed one. I knew my dad, and for any other man to attempt to fill that role would not have sat well with me. It would have felt forced even if he did genuinely want to be that father figure for me. I had tons of father figures, from uncles and older cousins to the fathers of my friends. It was always special to me to just observe the acts of a father figure.

When my grandfather passed, I had to see my father in his most vulnerable state. It was then that I realized why I needed to forgive my dad, because I'm not just my father's son; I am me! I am who He (God) says I am. I could finally appreciate God for creating the life I grew up to live.

I understood that it was no one's fault: not my mother's, not my father's, not mine, not anyone else's. It was just God's will for my life, and my dad only did what he knew to do.

MIKE PORTER

Mike B. Porter is a father, grandfather. and uncle. He is a former Marine, and a retired Police Officer, Sergeant of DeKalb County Police Department. His is a Tournament Bass fisherman andhe Loves traveling the world with his wife.

DOMESTIC VIOLENCE

My father was there for the younger years of my life. Those years, I really don't remember a lot of good when he was there. Domestic violence changed my view of my father. I have been filled with anger for many years, and I haven't forgotten it. I have not forgotten my mother and father fighting and the lingering effects it had on my mother. My mother made sure I was taken care of and was safe and fed. I had my great uncles and male cousins who demonstrated how I should act as a young man. I never felt sorry for myself at any time. My self-esteem was not damaged by my father not being present in the household. My father smoked marijuana on a regular basis, but I never felt the need to use drugs to dull the pain of my father not being the kind of father I needed him to be; instead, I used women and sex to escape my pain. I knew I did not want to do anything my father did. I wanted to be different than him.

When I saw my friends with their fathers and the great relationships they had, I felt sad sometimes. But, their fathers always treated me well, just like I was one of their own, and that made feel good.

Although my biological father was not in my life, I had a stepfather who was good to me and shared his time and experiences with me. He took me fishing and showed me how to be a good young black man. I had uncles and cousins who were also good examples for me. I decided when I was in my 30s to embrace the life that I was given and to live my life the best that I could with what I was given.

One thing I was clear about is that I wanted to be a better father to my children than my father was to me. I read self-help books on how to be a good parent. What I found was that sharing time with them has been one of the greatest highlights in my life. I made myself available to my children, and I spent as much time with them as I could. I tell my children that I love them often and that I will always be there for them no matter what.

A long time ago, I asked GOD to help me forgive my father for his shortcomings, to make me whole, and to make me a better man. Although I am not a church-going person, I am still a very spiritual person. I do believe in God. I pray for my wife, family, and others often.

At this point in my life, the greatest joys I have are being a great father to my children, enjoying retirement, and traveling with my wife without any restrictions.

CHARLES SEARCY

Charles Searcy was born in Boston MA to parents John and Barbara Searcy. He was a "dedicated solider to the streets" for over 40 years and never had a legal job until he was 50 years old. He started using drugs at the age of 12 and did not stop until he was 50 years old.

Charles now has a bachelor's degree, master's degree, his CASAC Certification, an HS-BCP Certification and is currently in school for his PhD. with a graduation date of November 2020.

A FATHER'S LOVE AND GUIDANCE IS KEY

My father was in my life, but not in the same way as many fathers. There were eight of us, and we all had the same father and mother. My mother loved this man and did not want to be without him, so she kind of took what she could get. He was a part-time husband and father. I don't think it was always like that, because I saw the pictures and heard the stories of how they were before I was born. I guess as time went on, my father's behavior changed due to his drug addiction. When it got worse, he was always in the streets! He only came home once in a while. I remember him loving us, but I also remember that my four sisters hated my dad. They wanted nothing to do with him because they needed him in a different way than my brothers and I. He wasn't around for them, and he became a stranger to them. He missed everything: school plays, basketball games, and pretty much anything that had to do with his children.

I still loved it when he would finally come to the house for however long he was there. It didn't really bother me too much, because I liked it when he came home! He always dressed nice and talked slick. Most of the time, he came home with his friends (which meant he was not staying). I watched them have so much fun laughing, drinking, and talking slang that I didn't understand. That's when I was young and unable to tell that my family was dysfunctional. Even though I didn't have a normal childhood, I do remember enjoying what I thought at the time were happy moments with my father.

Looking back, I realize that he wasn't happy; he was just entertaining and intoxicated! My dad had a serious drug habit. I remember getting up in the middle of the night to use the bathroom when I was 6 or 7, and I saw my dad using drugs for the first time. I didn't understand what was going on at the time. I just saw that he had a needle in his arm, and he was happy, so I didn't think anything bad about it. I just went back to bed. I didn't see my father often after that, only off and on and here and there.

Fast forward to when I turned 12, and I was in serious need of my father's love and guidance! I was young and starting to hang out with the wrong crowd. My mother didn't like my choice of friends at all and told me to stop hanging out with them. I didn't listen and still hung out with them every chance I got. To me, they were cool! I had the freedom to do what I wanted to do because my dad wasn't there to stop me. Unfortunately, it wasn't long before these same friends had me doing drugs, too! It seemed to be the thing to do! I thought back to when I saw my father doing it and how he didn't even attempt to hide it from me, and I also remembered how happy he was when I caught him. So, I said to myself, "If my father's doing it, and my best friend is doing it, then it must be alright. Not to mention, they were both so damn happy while doing it! Well, I tried it, and I liked it. It made me happy, too.

At least, I thought it was happiness. I now know it was just the drugs and not happiness. I had a problem, and I needed to keep it from my mother! I realized I was addicted when I became sick from not using the drugs, and my friends told me why I was so sick. That's when I began stealing for my habit to avoid feeling sick. My parents didn't know I was getting high until one day I was home playing hooky from school, and my father came to the house and saw me. I was so high I couldn't hide it. He was so mad that he hit me!

I was only 15 at the time, and ever since that day, our relationship changed. Now he looked out for me in the streets because he knew I was out there. He didn't want anything to happen to me. I guess he accepted the fact that I was into drugs and in the streets, and he thought it was best to look out for me. He taught my brother and me how to survive in the streets. Still in high school, I was often in trouble for stealing things from school to pay for my drug habit. I remember stealing money out of a teacher's wallet. When I got caught, my principal told me not to come back to school without my mother. Instead, I found my dad and told him what happened at school and that I couldn't come back without a parent. We both agreed not to tell my mother. The next morning, he picked me up for school. On the way to school my dad said to me, "The one thing I don't ever want you to do is lie to me. I don't care who you lie to. Just don't lie to me!"

I made a promise to my father that day to never lie to him, and he was always in my corner, taking up for me and keeping me out of trouble. I loved him for being there for me, whether I was right or wrong.

You see, my father was in my life, even though he didn't live with us. I realize he did not raise me. My mother did. Even though he looked out for me, it didn't stop me from getting into trouble and doing drugs. However, I will say that although I was a drug addict and a thief, I was taught to respect my elders and be very polite. For the most part, I was taught to be a good person, and I believe I owe that to my mother. Now that I'm older, I see that the only thing my father really taught me was how to get myself out of trouble. I loved him and always knew where to find him if I needed him for anything. People on the outside looking in may think we grew up without him, but I knew better. He may not have been the ideal father or what people may call a "good" father, but he was a good father in my eyes - not because he gave me money or spent a lot of time with me, but because he gave me good advice. To me, that was priceless.

I never blamed my father for the way I turned out, because I felt I did that to myself. My dad was good to me until the day he died. My mother never liked the relationship that my father and I had because she didn't want me to turn out like him. I suppose she just dealt with it because she didn't want to lose me to my father or the streets. In the end, I love both my mother and my father for the roles they played in my life.

As adults, we have to realize that our parents did the best they could by us. They only did what they were taught by their parents, good or bad. My father didn't have an example of what a good father was supposed to be because he didn't have his father in his life to show him. It was a ripple effect, and it caused me not to be the kind of father that my son needed me to be.

I didn't have a relationship with my son because I was using drugs and in and out of jail. One thing about jail, though: it gives you a lot of time to think. I thought about my life and what I needed to do to change it and make it better. I decided I wanted more out of my life, so I made the decision to go to school to see if it would help give me some direction. What I found was that I really liked school as an adult, and I liked the possibilities it offered me. Life threw me a lot of challenges, but I realized that everything we go through is to prepare us to help others. Today, I am proud to say that I will be graduating from college in October 2020 with my Phd in clinical psychology! I plan to help as many people as possible who are in similar situations to the ones I have been in. I am so thankful for the opportunity to reconnect with and develop a relationship with my son, who is now an amazing young man and is doing quite well for himself! At the end of the day, no matter what you have done or the kind of life you have lived, your choice to improve will always come back full circle and improve the lives of those you love as well!

BRANDON SPELLEN

Brandon is an amazing husband and father to 3 beautiful children. He has earned his BSN and RN degrees and currently works in the healthcare industry— committed and passionate about advocating for patient care. He loves to challenge himself through books, podcasts, and entrepreneurial endeavors.

MY DISAPPOINTMENT

Not having a father was very disappointing. My father was only in my life briefly, and I have no fond memories of him. I wish I could say I had some great memories of my dad, like throwing a ball around together or learning how to ride a bike, or some great life lessons I learned from him. Unfortunately, I do not have those memories. I realized at a young age, around 16 years old, that I should forget the idea of having a relationship with my dad. He was absent so much that it was almost like he never existed.

Thankfully, I didn't turn to drugs or any other substances to ease the pain. I never believed in escaping my problems by using drugs. I knew that it wouldn't make me feel any better. Not having him around made me feel unwanted and rejected. For a period of time, I felt like I didn't deserve love from others because my own father didn't seem to love me. It affected my ability to get close to women intimately, but as time went by and I grew up, I started to care less and less about my relationship with my father. Instead, I started to create a vision in my mind of how I wanted to be as a man, husband, and father. One thing I knew for sure was that I didn't want to be anything like him. I was determined to be a different and better man.

Having friends that had their fathers in their lives did make me want what they had, but I was never jealous. I appreciated the relationships that I did have and took notes. I wanted to replicate those same acts and feelings in my relationship with my own children. Much of what I have learned has been taken from what I have seen others do, especially my Uncle Colin, who I am thankful for. He has always been like a father to me. I've read many self-help books, and my relationship with God has had the greatest impact on who I've become.

I don't feel that my relationship with my father or lack thereof played a negative role in my relationship with my children. If anything, it caused me to consciously decide to be a better father. I never wanted my children to go through or feel like I did growing up. I want them to know that I would always be present in their lives.

I am so glad that I am saved and that I have a great relationship with God. Each day, I work on being better than I was the day before. If there was anything I could have done differently, it would have been to start a business and buy a home earlier in life to prepare for my family, because the things that bring me the greatest joy are my relationships with God, my wife, and my children.

LANCE SHARIFF

Lance Shariff is a loving son, brother, and father of three children. He is a former U.S. Army Officer. He is a Manager of Environmental Services at one of the major hospitals in Atlanta, GA. He enjoys life and all the possibilities God has for him.

IT WAS A COMMON PLACE

I grew up knowing who my father was, but he wasn't really in my life. I didn't hold any anger about him not being there. Not having our dads was commonplace with my friends and me, so it was somewhat normal. I have a few friends who had their dads in their lives, and I guess I did feel that they were blessed to have their fathers in their lives. I may not have had my dad, but I still had many male role models. I had my grandfather, uncles, and older cousins who were healthy role models. I am so glad that they were there. I also have a stepfather who I didn't truly appreciate for a long time like I should have. As I have gotten older, I can really appreciate the love, hard work, and teachings I received from him. I think these people in my life made up for my father's absence in a way, so I don't think my self-esteem and self-worth were really affected by my dad's absence. I was raised in a close knit family that gave us a lot of love.

I did use drugs. I can't say that it was ever directly related to the pain of my dad not being around, because I didn't really feel I was missing anything. I used drugs because it was the thing to do. I may have been also trying to escape the pain of just being a young black male in the inner city, dealing with poverty and crime. Now that I think about it, having my father around to help me with those feelings may have stopped me from doing a lot of the things that I found myself doing. I guess him not being there really did have an impact on me, because he wasn't there to talk me out of the poor choices I was making. If he had been there, maybe I could have made a change sooner.

At the time, I felt I was fine. I thought that as long as I'm a better father than my father, everything will be fine. I see now that just isn't true. Not having my dad made it hard to actually be a good dad, because I had no example. You don't realize that until you have to do it! I have two sons, and I know now that it's very important for young black males to have that positive father figure. Having your father there to mold and teach you is priceless. Just to be able to observe your father and how he navigates through life is helpful in going through your own life.

I think I started to see things differently after I turned 30 and had my own children. I'm starting to grow closer to God. Now, I see the importance of having a relationship with God, and it's made me wish I would have done more with and for my boys. I always communicated to them that I loved them, but I would have showed them better if I knew better, if I had that example of my own to follow. I also have a 5-year-old daughter, and I love being her dad. She brings me so much joy, but it also gives me a sense of guilt because I wasn't there for my boys the same way. But I am thankful to God that I have my children, and that it is never too late to be a good father and dad.

KEONE B. SHARIFF

Keone B. Shariff is a loving son, brother, and father. He is a graduate of the Dekalb County First Responders Academy and he serves as a fire fighter. He loves sports, his beautiful daughter, and all that he feels life has to offer him.

NOT FULLY UNDERSTANDING

I never fully understood the feelings I had about growing up without a father until recently. My father was never in my life. I have a stepdad (the father of two of my siblings) who was brought into my life when I was in the first grade. I still call him dad to this day, but the older I got, I started recognizing that although I called him dad, he couldn't have the love for me the way he had for his biological children. I understood and accepted that. Now that I am older, I can better comprehend how not having a relationship with my real father might have shaped me. My stepfather was there, as well as my grandfather, but my grandfather worked nights and wasn't able to spend the quality time with me that I needed. I still feel that my mother and grandmother mostly raised me. Being raised by mostly women, I think that I may be more sensitive emotionally than I would have been if I was raised by my father. I don't feel that I was properly taught about certain things that a young black man in America should know. I do believe that my father's absence has affected my self-esteem and confidence as a black man, but not to the point that I felt emotional pain that would have caused me to do things to harm myself, like the use of drugs. I think that may be because I have always had a really good support system, even without my dad being there. I also never felt jealous of my friends who had their fathers in their lives, because I have had the same friends since I was very young, and their families were like family to me.

When my daughter was born, I immediately fell in love with her and told myself that I could not imagine not being in her life to watch her grow. I wanted to teach her everything I knew about life. Wanting to be part of her life came easy for me. I was determined to be there for my daughter and to a have a strong and loving relationship with her.

I wanted to be a better father for her than my father was for me. Now that I'm older, I'm able to better understand my feelings and process them in a positive way, but I definitely feel that something is missing. I recently found out that I have three other siblings by my dad, ages 21, 15, and 13. Finding out about them was bittersweet; I was happy to know about them, but I also felt that the opportunity to know them and have a relationship with my them was stripped from me, because I didn't even know the man who creating us all.

I feel the presence of God in my life because my grandmother is a praying woman. I could feel the presence of her prayers covering me all through my life. However, I haven't been to church in a very long time. My mother stopped going, which stopped me from going. I thank God my grandmother continues to pour into me spiritually, which is why I still have belief in God and His higher power. I don't believe a person needs a physical place to worship God; you should worship God everywhere you go. I overall believe this way of thinking has allowed me to keep a level head and a sound mind. I know that God is within me, and just because I don't attend church, it doesn't mean that I am without God. I believe that I am still able to find joy no matter what. I find joy in knowing that I come from a family that loves me and my child.

One of the things that brought great joy was in my junior year of high school. My grandmother drove up to my school with a brand new car. I can remember saying to her, "Wow, this a nice car."

She pulled out the keys and said, "Congratulations! It is yours."

I remember my friends saying, "Wow! I wish I had a grandmother like that!"

My grandparents have played an important role in my life. For that, I am ever grateful. I also find great joy in the work that I do as a firefighter, though if I had the chance to do it all over, I would have gone into it right out of high school, because I love it! I also find joy in my friendships that I have had since I was a kid. We play ball together and enjoy our leisure time playing videogames and just having fun. I think having fun and relaxing are an important part of having a balanced life, and I am glad that I have that.

GILBERT WHITE

Gilbert White is a Retired Regional Manager for the Mass Department of Public Health Bureau of Substance Abuse/HIV AIDS Bureau.

An avid tennis player, loves politics, saxophonist, entertainer, public speaker, and clotheshorse.

Gilbert has three adult children and three grandchildren.

I FELT ABANDONED WITHOUT AN IDENTITY

As a child, I felt abandoned and without an identity of who I was. Having an absent father left me empty, sad, angry, and confused. I felt like a lost child, which affected my self-esteem. I believe it's why I started using drugs and living a life of crime. It's also why I dealt with various women. I was self-medicating to deal with the pain, and the women helped me not feel so alone. I think I followed in my father's footsteps when it came to his criminal history. Maybe that was me trying to be like my dad in some way, shape, or form. It was embarrassing not having a dad. When I saw my friends who did have their dads, I felt jealous and envious of them. We all need to have a dad, and not having mine left a big void in my life. I watched fathers on TV, and I heard stories from kids who had their dads, but I had no real role model of my own. I always felt that I was looked upon negatively because of my seemingly dysfunctional family. Some of my friends' parents wouldn't even let their children play with me. I had a lot of mixed feelings that I couldn't understand at that time. Even though he wasn't there, I still had a love for this man that I didn't really know. I painted a picture of who and what my father was from what my mother and other family members told me about him.

I told myself at a young age that I would make sure that I raised my children differently! I promised myself that I would always be in their lives and be there for them. I wanted them to know that they could always count on me. I wasn't going to allow them to experience what I went through as a child. I was determined that not only were they going to have a father, but that they would also have a good dad in their lives who loved them and cared about them. Once I decided to stop using drugs and living a life of crime, God began to change all aspects of my life.

There are no guarantees about how life turns out, but I do believe that if I had a father in my life, things could've been better and different for me. I've always been a spiritual person. My belief in God and my family ancestors watching over me played a big part in my recovery. God has known me from the beginning and has always known my heart. I wouldn't be the man I am today if I hadn't gone through all I did, so there's not much I would change in my life, with the exception of pursuing my education and having my parents in my life. Growing up, being smart wasn't cool, so I dumbed myself down so that I could fit in. Now that I know better, I can teach my children better. Having my children, grandchildren, family, friends, and a partner in my life has allowed me to have a profound love for myself and for God, who gave me life and watches over us all.

KIM ELLOCK

Kim Ronald Ellcock was born and raised in Cambridge, MA. He is a retired Mutual Funds Manager. In 1986 he married his soulmate, Kim and together they raised their two children: Kimberly (31) and Anthony a.k.a., Kim-Anthony (18) in Brockton, MA where they still reside happily married. He is also a proud grandfather of two grandchildren: Kimora (11) and Kimron (2) who are his pride and joy. Affectionately known as Kim-Boy, he is very proud to have children and grandchildren who are his namesake. A true family man, he enjoys being the patriarch of the Kim family and plans to enjoy the rest of his retired life spending time with his family.

THE MAN GOD HAS CALLED ME TO BE

My father was an alcoholic, which ended up taking his life. I was 12 years old when my dad passed away, but up to that point my father was very present in my life. After his death, I recalled beginning to miss him. I am glad that I did not allow his death to affect my self-esteem, which I am thankful for to this day!

Family is everything to me I am so glad that I had aunts that loved me like my Auntie Ruthie and Audrey, which were my fathers sisters. Because I had so many positive role models in my life, I did not have any painful feelings about my father not being in my life. I am so thankful my best friend's father always treated me like I was his son, which made me feel like I belonged and was loved. In addition, my older brothers and older cousins and uncles would take me to basketball games, fishing and various outings. Even though I had these amazing men around me I missed not having my father around. I would have loved having my father in my life, so that we could have built a great father-son relationship!

One of the things, I was determined to do was to build a relationship with my children by always being a hands-on father from the time they were born. I attended their sporting events, school programs and made sure we had a family vacation every year. I wanted to make sure I was there for them, like my older relatives were for me. My goal was to be a role model for my children, nieces and nephews. When I think back, I wanted to set standards for the man my son should strive to be. My motives for my daughter were similar, in that I wanted the standard I set to be the minimum requirements she should look for in her husband. I was determined to be physically and emotionally present and involved in their lives.

When I was in high school, I was determined to be strong and work hard to be all that God has called me to be. My father was not around to see me grow and become a great man, husband, father and grandfather and I have a big hole in my heart—missing my father. But through it all, God has blessed me with a beautiful wife of 33 years. She is what I call a true partner. She has loved me through it all, and for that I am so thankful for her. Although life throws many blocks in our way, I would have to say that I would not change my journey for anything. I love my life and I believe that all things work together for our good. My greatest joy is being married to my soulmate, being a father and grandfather and the man that God has called me to be!

JOHN LEWIS

Originally Published in the NY Times. John Lewis wrote this essay shortly before his death, to be published upon the day of his funeral.

Together, you can redeem the soul of our nation. Though I am gone, I urge you to answer the highest calling of your heart and stand up for what you truly believe.

While my time here has now come to an end, I want you to know that in the last days and hours of my life you inspired me. You filled me with hope about the next chapter of the great American story when you used your power to make a difference in our society. Millions of people motivated simply by human compassion laid down the burdens of division. Around the country and the world you set aside race, class, age, language and nationality to demand respect for human dignity.
That is why I had to visit Black Lives Matter Plaza in Washington, though I was admitted to the hospital the following day. I just had to see and feel it for myself that, after many years of silent witness, the truth is still marching on.

Emmett Till was my George Floyd. He was my Rayshard Brooks, Sandra Bland and Breonna Taylor. He was 14 when he was killed, and I was only 15 years old at the time. I will never ever forget the moment when it became so clear that he could easily have been me. In those days, fear constrained us like an imaginary prison, and troubling thoughts of potential brutality committed for no understandable reason were the bars.

Though I was surrounded by two loving parents, plenty of brothers, sisters and cousins, their love could not protect me from the unholy oppression waiting just outside that family circle. Unchecked, unrestrained violence and government-sanctioned terror had the power to turn a simple stroll to the store for some Skittles or an innocent morning jog down a lonesome country road into a nightmare. If we are to survive as one unified nation, we must discover what so readily takes root in our hearts that could rob Mother Emanuel Church in South Carolina of her brightest and best, shoot unwitting concertgoers in Las Vegas and choke to death the hopes and dreams of a gifted violinist like Elijah McClain.

Like so many young people today, I was searching for a way out, or some might say a way in, and then I heard the voice of Dr. Martin Luther King Jr. on an old radio. He was talking about the philosophy and discipline of nonviolence. He said we are all complicit when we tolerate injustice. He said it is not enough to say it will get better by and by. He said each of us has a moral obligation to stand up, speak up and speak out. When you see something that is not right, you must say something. You must do something. Democracy is not a state. It is an act, and each generation must do its part to help build what we called the Beloved Community, a nation and world society at peace with itself.

Ordinary people with extraordinary vision can redeem the soul of America by getting in what I call good trouble, necessary trouble. Voting and participating in the democratic process are key. The vote is the most powerful nonviolent change agent you have in a democratic society. You must use it because it is not guaranteed. You can lose it.

You must also study and learn the lessons of history because humanity has been involved in this soul-wrenching, existential struggle for a very long time. People on every continent have stood in your shoes, though decades and centuries before you. The truth does not change, and that is why the answers worked out long ago can help you find solutions to the challenges of our time. Continue to build union between movements stretching across the globe because we must put away our willingness to profit from the exploitation of others.

Though I may not be here with you, I urge you to answer the highest calling of your heart and stand up for what you truly believe. In my life I have done all I can to demonstrate that the way of peace, the way of love and nonviolence is the more excellent way. Now it is your turn to let freedom ring.

When historians pick up their pens to write the story of the 21st century, let them say that it was your generation who laid down the heavy burdens of hate at last and that peace finally triumphed over violence, aggression and war. So I say to you, walk with the wind, brothers and sisters, and let the spirit of peace and the power of everlasting love be your guide.

WORDS TO ENCOURAGE YOU ON YOUR JOURNEY

Repeat them every morning!

Philippians 4:6-7
I will not be anxious about anything; instead in everything through prayer and petition with thanksgiving, I will tell my request to God.
In the name and through the power of Jesus Christ!

John 16:23-24
My Father will give me whatever I ask in His name. I will ask and I will receive, and my joy will be completed.
In the name and through the power of Jesus Christ!

Proverbs 10:22
The blessings of the Lord make me rich, and He adds no sorrow with it.
In the name and through the power of Jesus Christ!

Psalm 32:8
The Lord will instruct me and teach me in the way I should go. He will council and watch over me. He will guide me with His eyes.
In the name and through the power of Jesus Christ!

Jeremiah 31:3
In a far off land the Lord will manifest Himself to me. He will say to me (put your name here), I have loved you with everlasting love. That is why I continue to be faithful to you.
In the name and through the power of Jesus Christ!

Ephesians 6:16
I will take up the shield of faith with which I can extinguish all the flaming arrows of the enemy!
In the name and through the power of Jesus Christ!

Matthew 6:33
I will seek first the kingdom of God and His righteousness. When I do that, all things shall be added to me.
In the name and through the power of Jesus Christ!

Proverbs 3:5-6
I will trust in the Lord with all my heart and lean not on my own understanding; I will acknowledge you in all your ways, for it is You that will make my paths straight.
In the name and through the power of Jesus Christ!

Psalm 139:14
I praise You because I am fearfully and wonderfully made; by you, your works are wonderful, and I know them full well.
In the name and through the power of Jesus Christ!

Romans 12:2
I will not be conformed to the patterns of this world, but I will be transformed by the renewal of my mind. Then I will know God's good and pleasing and perfect will for my life.
In the name and through the power of Jesus Christ!

Psalm 37:7
I wait patiently on the Lord. I wait confidently for Him.
In the name and through the power of Jesus Christ!

Psalm 21:6
For You grant me lasting blessings. You gave me great joy by allowing me into your presence!
In the name and through the power of Jesus Christ!

Hebrews 4:16
Therefore, I will confidently approach the throne of favor, to receive mercy and favor whenever I need help.
In the name and through the power of Jesus Christ!

Please contact Nora at info@bwotmfg.com for speaking engagements.

For more information about Business Women on the Move for God and other products please visit at www.bwotmfg.com.